THE

Traditional

IRISH

Wedding

Bridget Nancy Margaret O'Flaherty emigrated to the United States to marry the man she had met on a blind date. Today, Mr. & Mrs. Russell Haggerty both work out of the 'money pit' - an antique Queen Anne residence in Cincinnati, Ohio, where they raised a family, dropped out of corporate America, and now pursue freelance careers in consulting, writing and whatever else will keep the lights on.

This book is dedicated to Russ, my anam cara of over forty years who helped see it through to completion, who read every word over and over, and who gave me support and encouragement every step of the way. If not for him, I would never have finished it. Thank you, Russ. My love and gratitude always.

THE
Traditional
IRISH
Wedding

Bridget J. Haggerty

Irish Culture and Customs

Published by Irish Culture and Customs
Cincinnati OH
www.irishcultureandcustoms.com

Reprinted and distributed in
the United States of America
in 2007 by
North American Celtic Buyers Association
27 Addison Avenue
Rutherford, NJ 07070
www.CelticBuyers.com
Tel: (201) 842-9922
Fax: (201) 804-9143

Second edition published in 2004 by Irish Books and Media, Inc.
Minneapolis, MN USA

First published in 1999 by Wolfhound Press, Dublin, Ireland
and Irish Books and Media, Minneapolis, MN USA
Library of Congress control number: 2004105571
ISBN-13: 978-0-9798765-0-9
ISBN-10: 0-9798765-0-8

10 9 8 7 6 5 4 3 2 1

Claddagh Ring Symbol: Drawing by Russ Haggerty
Cover Photograph: Russ Haggerty
Cover Design: Patrick Michael Redmond, M.A., Patrick Redmond Design
Printed in the USA by Range Printing, Brainerd, Minnesota

CONTENTS

Acknowledgements

Introduction

INFORMATION AND RESOURCES

ACKNOWLEDGEMENTS

Think where man's glory most begins and ends
And say my glory was I had such friends
W.B. Yeats

When the first edition of this book was published in 1999, I wrote that I had been blessed with an incredible abundance of support from family and friends. That is still the case. You know who you are. I also hope you know how much I treasure each and every one of you. May white light surround you always.

In this expanded and updated version, I would like to thank Linda Schmidt for sharing her vow renewal celebration; Anne Lanier of Anne Lanier Weddings for her invaluable information on getting married in Ireland; Aideen Barrett for the additions and corrections to the Irish words and phrases; and Nancy Larkin Rau of the Bunratty Mead & Liqueur Co. for her outstanding promotional efforts on my behalf. I am also deeply grateful to my former publisher - the now regrettably out of business Irish Books & Media - for making a second edition possible, and also the North American Celtic Buyers Association for funding this reprint.

Friends and acquaintances who encouraged my efforts when working on the first book are still thought of very fondly: Terri Abare, Siobhan Campbell, Barbara Harding, Penny Cappel, Jane FitzGerald, and the members of the wedding party who embraced the idea of an Irish celebration with joyful exuberance.

And finally, I'd like to acknowledge Seamus Cashman of Wolfhound Press who has since sold the business and is now enjoying his retirement. From him, I learned patience, respect for 'Irish time' and how to keep the faith.

The publisher is happy to also acknowledge with thanks the following, for permission to reproduce copyright material: Mercier Press Ltd. for extracts from *In My Father's Time* by Eamon Kelly, 'The Way Matches Were Made' from *The Man from Cape Clear* by Conchúr Ó Siocháin and 'Haste to the Wedding' from *In Ireland Long Ago* by Kevin Danaher; Peters, Fraser & Dunlop for the extract from 'The Maiden's Plight' by Brian Merriman, translated by Frank O'Connor. Thanks also to the following who gave permission to use their own recipes in this book: Darina Allen for recipes from *The Festive Food of Ireland* (Roberts Rinehart Publishers), Georgina Campbell for recipes from *The Best of Irish Bread & Baking* (Wolfhound Press, Dublin) and *Classic Irish Recipes* (Sterling, New York), and Margaret Johnson for her recipes from *Cooking with Irish Spirits* (Wolfhound Press, Dublin). 'The Irish Wedding Song,' traditional, Ian Betteridge/Noel Healy, *The Wedding Song Book* (Kells Music Publications, New York, also Waltons Manufacturing Ltd. Dublin). Where we have been unable to contact any copyright holder, we would be grateful if they would write the publisher.

INTRODUCTION

I'm 100% Irish and have never lived in Ireland. My father was a Galway man, reared in the Claddagh. My mother was a Dubliner from Upper Artane. I was born and raised in England.

While my husband, my children and my life are American, my dream is to someday live in Ireland. It's a longing I didn't know existed until I went back after forty years. The first time was for a funeral and I was very young - just turned ten. The next time - this time - was, in many ways, a return to my roots. What I discovered was a spiritual renewal and a realization that in my heart of hearts, Ireland is my home.

Before taking the trip, I had already begun work on this book. The inspiration for it came about while planning our daughter's wedding. After the engagement was announced, mother and daughter did the usual thing - everything in our lives unrelated to getting married came to a screeching halt. The only thing that had momentum for either one of us was planning the perfect wedding. And what came out of those initial planning sessions was that she wanted a ceremony and reception that would reflect her Irish heritage.

An Irish Wedding - in America? It made sense to begin my research by asking a friend who was married in Dublin to compare her celebration with weddings in the States. I was surprised and disappointed when she said that there really wasn't that much of a difference - contemporary Irish weddings use the same ceremonial music and follow the usual rituals. But it was not always so.

Irish folklore is filled with fascinating customs, superstitions and traditions. However, as I was to learn from my recent journey home, the old ways are fast being forgotten.

In Blarney Woolen Mills, I ran into a young family whose daughter had just made her First Holy Communion. They were there to buy her a gift and I assumed it would be an Aran Isle sweater. I'd read about the custom during my research, but when I mentioned it to her parents, they had never heard of it. Perhaps it's only a tradition along Ireland's west coast? Along the same lines, I wanted to buy Aran sweaters for my sons in the O'Flaherty pattern - my father's name. According to what I'd read, sea-faring families adopted a unique pattern or group of stitches which eventually became identified with their name and from where they came. Should anything happen to the fishermen at sea, people would know who they were. I asked in places from Connemara to Cork and even sought the advice of a professional Aran Isle knitter but not one person knew what I was talking about. After the first edition of this book was published, I found out why: it's a myth! There's no evidence of the distinctive Aran sweaters before the 1930s, and in fact, the only garments that appear to have been knit on the islands prior to the 20th century are socks! Apparently, the 'drowned man' story was created by a marketing genius who was very familiar with the various stitches and their meanings. He or she also knew that families and even entire villages favored certain sequences. So, yes, up to a point, you could perhaps identify a man by his sweater. One thing led to another, and it wasn't long before people like myself began making the mistake of pursuing their family pattern - similar to a person with Scottish roots looking for their tartan. While I was a bit disappointed to discover an O'Flaherty Aran doesn't exist, I can't say the same for the sweaters we did end up buying - they are among the most warm and comfortable garments we own.

Today, Ireland is still as beautiful as ever, and the inhabitants just as warm and friendly. But the difference between now, and thirty or forty years ago, is that there's an eagerness to leave the past behind and move forward. The country is indeed making incredible strides but as Ireland becomes more modern, her people - most notably the young ones - are less interested in much that appeals to the tourists - the music, the language, the history. Even in the pubs, it's not often that you hear traditional music, except during tourist season. I thought about my parents and what they would think. And it was as hard for me as it would have been for them to accept that their days are gone. Now, it's for the visitors that the locals play a favorite tune. And *The Minstrel Boy* is considered such a cliché, one hesitates to ask. But I did anyway.

With all this in mind, I felt compelled to include as many Irish elements as I could in our daughter's wedding. Ironic as it might seem, it would be more Irish than if she exchanged her vows in Ireland. From the outset, it quickly became apparent that it wasn't going to be easy; but I was determined to at least explore the possibilities.

What I was looking for was a single source that would tell me all about Irish customs, traditions, music, and feasting. I searched bookstores, combed the library, and ended up buying or borrowing a ton of books from which I gleaned snippets here and there. What I never could find was a single book that described all of the elements that go into an *old-fashioned* Irish wedding celebration plus background information on superstitions, the ancient laws, and anything else relating to courtship, weddings, and marriage in Ireland. When it became obvious that such a book did not exist, I decided to write it myself.

So here's the result. Within the following pages, you'll find suggestions for music, recipes for your reception and ideas for attire, flowers and decor - and as much as I could find on Irish weddings - the way they were. Even if you apply just a few recommendations, or use them to generate your own ideas, your day should be delightfully different - but perhaps the best part is that it will echo our ancestral customs and help keep them from fading into memory.

As long as there are Irish folk, and Irish wit and laughter,
You'll both be wished the best of luck for now and ever after!

BRIDGET HAGGERTY
Sláinte!

As young Rory and Moreen were talking,
How Shrove Tuesday was drawing near;
For the tenth time he asked her to marry;
But says she, 'Time enough till next year.'
Then ochone I'm going to Skellig
O Moreen what will I do?
Tis the woeful road to travel
And how lonesome I'll be without you.

St. Patrick's Day was once considered to be the
luckiest day in the year to marry, and according to an old
Irish saying, 'November is the time to wed,
the harvest's in and it's cold in bed.'

There are twelve months in all the year,
as I heard my mamma say,
Two of them I would choose to love,
the months of June and May.
These are the months I choose to love,
when the red roses spring,
And the other months I would choose to wed,
when the small birds sweetly sing.

In County Wexford, if a couple is described as 'mighty coonagh'
they're going strong or walking out.

What Irish magpies foretold: One for sorrow;
two for mirth; three for a wedding; four for a birth.

Wait till you're eighteen to marry and
don't be spoiling your growth.

1

D'REIR AN SEANA CHULTUR
ACCORDING TO CUSTOM

Storytellers, authors, poets, and movie-makers have attempted to capture the Irish rites of romance and from these sources have been gleaned some of the most colorful examples of how couples once wooed and wed.

In ancient Ireland and up until the arrival of the Normans in the twelfth century, the rules regarding the marriage ritual came under the Brehon Laws, which evolved from the customs of the early tribes. Under the law, marriage seemed to be a somewhat casual affair: A couple could marry 'for one year certain' and either one could withdraw after one year if they wished, but the regulations surrounding the marriage contract were far more complex.

The laws determined exactly those who may contract a proper marriage and under what conditions. The Irish word for marriage is *lánamus* which can be translated fairly accurately as a social connection for the purposes of procreation. Thus, a barren man could not make a contract, and this condition could also be used to annul a marriage if it became apparent that the husband could not father a child. Others who could not enter into a contract were:

An unarmed man: A euphemism for impotency

A man in Holy Orders: A direct influence of the Christian Church, which strictly enforced the law of celibacy after the fifth century

A rockman: A picturesque term used to describe someone who had no land

A very obese man: This was because he would find it difficult to perform his procreative duty

A claonán: This means a perverted little wretch, a severe term to describe a man who discloses his woman's intimate secrets. By his indiscreet blabbing, a *claonán* would forfeit the right to marriage or invalidate any contract already in effect

A Churchman: This meant a bishop. Brehon lawyers loved mystical numbers such as seven and by adding Churchmen to the listing, they achieved their objective.

While a comparable listing of laws for women couldn't be found, certain qualities were traditionally sought by prospective husbands: a pleasant speaking voice, the ability to sing sweetly, skill at embroidery, wisdom and preferably, virginity. In pre-Christian Ireland, sexual experience would not have precluded the making of a match.

Once it was determined that a prospective husband and wife could make a contract, their families then addressed the business aspects of the union. The agenda generally included:

Coibche ~ the prospective husband paid a *coibche* to the girl's father, who then divided it with the head of the tribe. The *coibche* was paid each year for a total of 21 years, if the marriage lasted that long. In the second year, the wife kept a third of the amount for herself, while her father and the head of the tribe divided the remainder. As years went by, the wife kept a larger part. At the end of the 21 years, she would have amassed a considerable amount of personal property that would enable her to live independently if the union were dissolved.

Tionól ~ a wedding present to the bride from her friends and acquaintances and consisted of cattle - the chief wealth of the time. It was divided between the bride and her father, the father getting one third and his daughter the rest. Interestingly, at one time in Ireland, valuables other than cattle were called 'dry money'.

Tionchor ~ household goods given to the bride as a means of livelihood and support.

Tionnscra ~ a payment made to the father of the bride when she was from outside her husband's *tuath* - a region ruled by a king. It consisted of easily transportable wealth such as articles of gold, silver, copper, and brass.

In the old days, it was customary for the eldest girl in a family to marry first and her sisters, according to age, afterwards. It was also the custom that at the great fairs where contracts were often made, the young boys and girls of marriageable age were kept apart until the business at hand was concluded.

Centuries ago, before wedding ceremonies moved from the bride's house to the church steps, and finally into the church itself, the joining of a couple was often conducted outdoors in a place of mystical significance. On the island of Cape Clear, located off the west coast of County Cork, there is a townland called Comillane where you'll find four *gallawns* or pillarstones. Of the four, one is known as *Cloch na Gealluna* - 'The Trysting Stone'. It has a hole right through it and in pre-Christian times, a couple would join hands through the stone and in the presence of the local king, they would wed. Similarly, at the seventh-century Kilmaolcheader church near Dingle, County Kerry, stands an ogham pillar with a circular opening near the top. Legend has it that a couple is engaged if they join hands through the opening.

Then, as now, the road to romance and eventual marriage was never smooth, but ancient Ireland was a place where people believed in the power of charms. One of the charms requires that freshly-churned butter be placed on a new-made dish and presented to the prospective lover in a location where there would be a mill, a stream, and a tree - all symbols of endurance. The man would then say very softly: "Oh woman, loved by me, mayst thou give me thy heart, thy soul and body." (A variation of this custom was for the groom to present the butter to his bride and then he would say the words as a prayer, ending with an Amen.) Another charm for love is said three times in secret by the bride over a drink to be given to her betrothed: "This is the charm I set for love: A woman's charm of love and desire; you for me and I for thee and for none else; your face to mine and your hand turned away from all others."

Young maidens in old Ireland attempted all manner of techniques and devices to attract a suitor, as described in the following poem written by Brian Merriman, an eighteenth-century schoolmaster from County Clare. This version, translated by Frank O'Connor, appears in *The Book of Irish Verse*, ed. John Montague:

THE MAIDEN'S PLIGHT

I fasted three canonical hours
To try and come round the heavenly powers;
I washed my shift where the stream was deep
To hear a lover's voice in sleep;
Often I swept the woodstack bare,
Burned bits of my frock, my nails, my hair,
Up the chimney stuck the flail,
Slept with a spade, without avail;
Hid my wool in the limekiln late
And my distaff behind the churchyard gate;
I had flax on the road to halt coach or carriage
And haycocks stuffed with heads of cabbage.
And night and day on the proper occasions
invoked Old Nick and all his legions;
But t'was all no good and I'm broken hearted
For here I'm back at the place I started;
And this is the cause of all my tears
I am fast in the rope of the rushing years,
With age and need in lessening span,
And death beyond, and no hope of a man.

Was there an easier way? Well, according to yet another old tradition, all the poor maiden had to do was go to Lough Derg nine times and she would find a husband. Lough Derg is located in County Donegal and it's where St. Patrick is said to have fasted for 40 days. Today, thousands of pilgrims still make the journey, transported by boats which take them from the shore to Station Island, about a half-mile out. For three days, pilgrims eat dry bread, and drink black tea, travel barefoot, sleep in spartan conditions, and spend their waking hours in prayer. Whether or not modern day meditants go there with the intention of landing a spouse, go there they do.

> ### OLD IRISH PROPOSALS
>
> *Would you like to hang your washing next to mine?*
>
> *Would you like to be buried with my people?*
>
> *Live in my heart and pay no rent.*

In more recent times, a woman's status in Ireland, as in many other places throughout the world, has not been as lofty as it once was. Under the Brehon laws, a marriage between two equal partners was looked upon with great favor because it simplified the relationship. The wife is described as *comthigeran* which means co-lord, and both she and her husband were required to jointly provide food for the great festivals and collaborate equally in the buying of breeding cattle, the collection of household effects, and the fattening of pigs. Any horse or ox which had outlived its usefulness could not be sold without consultation and the price had to be used for the benefit of both. In fact, all the details of life were cared for meticulously by the Brehon laws so as to protect the rights of the wife against any exploitation by her husband or his family.

Over the years, and especially after Christianity came to Ireland, other customs developed. In County Limerick, during the matchmaking festivals which were held around harvest time, available bachelors always wore the shamrock and the houses of eligible girls were painted blue. In County Donegal, when a man wanted to marry a particular girl, he and a friend went to her house and when the door was opened, he'd throw his cap into the house. If the cap was thrown back out, it meant she wasn't interested. In County Westmeath, when a man and woman ' jumped the bezum' (twig or broom), it meant they were going to marry; and in County Waterford, a custom still surviving is that of single girls hopping around the Metal Man, an iron monster that points to the treacherous rocks in Tramore Bay. Hopping around three times ensures marriage within a year.

The main season for marrying used to be from Christmas to Lent, so that come Shrovetide, (the three days: Shrove Sunday, Shrove Monday, and Shrove Tuesday, preceding Ash Wednesday), a great deal of persuasion and pressure was brought to bear on single people to take the plunge. The first Sunday after Shrove Tuesday (the first Sunday in Lent), was known as 'Chalk Sunday' and it was then that bachelors who should have been married were marked with a heavy streak of chalk on the back of their 'Sunday coats.' This trick was perpetrated by boys who carried bits of chalk in their pockets and lay in wait for their victims. The marking was done while the congregation was assembling for Mass and after the trick was played, the young chalkers ran for their lives, always laughing and often singing the words of some suitable doggerel, such as 'And you are not married though Lent has come.'

Directly related to the escapades of Chalk Sunday was the distribution of the 'Skellig Lists'. Off the coast of County Kerry lie the Skellig Islands - 'the last parish before Brooklyn.' On the Great Skellig Rock are the ruins of St. Finnian's monastery and all those who should have been married before Lent were supposed to make a pilgrimage there on Shrove Tuesday night. Research indicates that this particular ritual was probably just make-believe, but the Skellig Lists were as real as the chalk marks on an unsuspecting bachelor's back. According to custom, a local bard would compose a jocose rhyming catalog of all the unmarried men and women and this list would be circulated on Shrove Tuesday and for some time after, causing much discomfort and embarrassment to all those singled out for still being unwed. Do you suppose that the phrase 'singled out' is derived from this old Irish custom?

Indirectly related to Chalk Sunday and the Skellig Lists is a game called 'Skellicking.' Apparently, boys in the city of Cork still play it today. On the eve of Shrove Tuesday, they chase after a girl with a rope, two boys to a rope, and attempt to capture her. If she is caught, the boys try to encircle her with the rope and pretend to 'take her off to the Skelligs.'

Long after the Brehon Laws had passed into antiquity, many Irish weddings were still arranged like business deals and little thought was given to romance and courtship. In fact, it was not unheard of for the couple to meet for the first time only a week before their marriage. Two or three nights before the wedding day, the groom would arrive at the bride's house for a celebration. Friends and neighbors of the bride's family would be invited over for dancing, drinking and singing which often would last well into the night and even into the next day.

GOOD-LUCK SIGNS AND PORTENTS

Inevitably, in addition to customs and traditions, superstitions associated with weddings became a part of Irish culture. Grooms used to give 'luck money' to the bride's parents to bring good fortune on their house. A throwback to the old Brehon laws, (as was the bride's fortune which was given by the bride's parents), it often averaged more than a hundred pounds. Over a century ago, that would have been a huge amount of money. There was a great deal of pride attached to the amount of a fortune since the respect for a bride and groom often hinged on its value.

Good luck was also taken into account when a couple chose the day they would exchange vows:

Monday for health,

Tuesday for wealth,

Wednesday the best day of all,

Thursday for losses,

Friday for crosses and

Saturday no day at all.

As for the months, the Cashel lexicographer of the ninth century, Cormac Mac Cullenan, observed that November was the favorite time for a wedding. In those days, this made a lot of sense because Ireland was a pastoral civilization and by November, the summer and fall work was completed, the cows and their attendants had returned from their pastures, and since the harvest was in, the wealth of the people was at its greatest. However, if November isn't your first choice, here is Irish poetic opinion for the rest of the year:

Marry when the year is new, always loving, kind and true.

When February birds do mate, you may wed, nor dread your fate.

If you wed when March winds blow, joy and sorrow both you'll know.

Marry in April when you can, joy for maiden and for man.

Marry in the month of May, you will surely rue the day.
Marry when June roses blow, over land and sea you'll go.
They who in July do wed, must labor always for their bread.
Whoever wed in August be, many a change are sure to see.

Marry in September's shine, your living will be rich and fine.
If in October you do marry, love will come but riches tarry.
If you wed in bleak November, only joy will come, remember.
When December's showers fall fast, marry and true love will last.

In addition to the days and months, many signs and portents were observed on the wedding day - nothing could be allowed to cast a shadow over what was considered one of the most important community events:

♥ A fine day meant good luck, especially if the sun shone on the bride
♥ A day of rain foretold hardship
♥ It was unlucky to marry on a Saturday
♥ Those who married in harvest would spend all their lives gathering
♥ A man should always be the first to wish joy to the bride, never a woman
♥ It was lucky to hear a cuckoo on the wedding morning, or to see three magpies
♥ To meet a funeral on the road meant bad luck and if there was a funeral procession planned for that day, the wedding party always took a different road
♥ The wedding party should always take the longest road home from the church
♥ It was bad luck if a glass or cup were broken on the wedding day
♥ A bride and groom should never wash their hands in the same sink at the same time - it's courting disaster if they do
♥ It was said to be lucky if you married during a growing moon and a flowing tide
♥ When leaving the church, someone must throw an old shoe over the bride's head so she will have good luck
♥ It's bad luck if newly-weds don't meet a man on their way home from the church
♥ If the bride and groom sprinkle a few drops of whiskey on the ground as they enter the reception, it's said to help ward off evil and keep them from harm all the days of their lives

♥ If the bride's mother-in-law breaks a piece of wedding cake on the bride's head as she enters the house after the ceremony, they will be friends for life.

While many of the old ways are long gone, some have become part of today's rituals. In tenth-century Ireland, a couple would walk to church together on their wedding day. If the people of the parish approved of their union, they would throw rice, pots and pans, brushes and other household goods - no doubt, an early harbinger of today's showers. And similar to our tradition of starting a hope chest, wealthy Irish households of centuries ago would set aside a special chest for a daughter's wedding clothes and marriage linens.

For a thoroughly entertaining look at Irish courtship, consider renting or buying a video of *The Quiet Man*. Produced in 1951 and directed by John Ford, it tells the story of a professional boxer who retires from the ring to return to his childhood home, intent on buying back his mother's cottage. He meets a young woman, falls in love and proposes marriage. At one point, right after Sunday Mass, the village matchmaker scolds the would-be-suitor for "playing patty fingers in the Holy Water, a privilege reserved for courting couples and then only when the banns have been read." To make everything official, the matchmaker escorts the young man to the girl's house to ask permission to go 'walking out' (woo). What follows is chaperoned courtship, and central to the plot, a veritable Dublin donnybrook over the bride's fortune, which almost ruins the marriage. Fortunately, the story does have a happy ending.

CHARMS

*To predict a prospective groom's fidelity, a maiden
would boil an egg hard, remove the yolk, fill the cavity with salt,
then eat it. She then had to go to bed without drinking
anything or speaking. If her man appeared in a dream, and offered
water to quench her thirst, he would be unfaithful.*

*Very old nutshell charm: Take two chestnuts and silently name
them for yourself and your lover. Place them on the bars
of the fire grate and watch. If they burn quietly and steadily,
you will gain a faithful love. If his chestnut should jump away
from yours, you will be disappointed, and if your own
chestnut should move, your love will pass.*

2

IRISH COURTSHIP
AND WEDDING STORIES

LOVE & MARRIAGE

At the bride's house, both bride and groom were presented with a plate of oatmeal and salt. Each took three mouthfuls as a protection against the power of the evil eye. This customary ritual was, for the most part, merely an indication that the festivities were about to begin.

For the daughter of a fairly well-off farmer, the ceremony would most likely have taken place in the barn in order to comfortably accommodate a large number of guests. Imagine a long table extending the length of the barn laden with a huge feast. The bride's mother and her friends serve the guests while musicians play traditional airs. When everyone has eaten, the table is cleared away and as soon as the cloth is removed, the priest rises to perform the ceremony. Guests crowd around the table so that they might have the honor of having their names recorded as witness. The ceremony ends with the priest commanding the groom to 'give your wife the kiss of peace.'

From *Of Irish Ways* by Mary Murray Delaney

SHROVETIDE

Many is the young woman came back - well she wouldn't be young after ten years in New York, but young enough! - and married a farmer, bringing with her a fortune of three or four hundred dollars. Then, if the farmer had an idle sister, and by idle I don't mean out of work, the fortune was for her. Then she could marry another farmer, or the man of her fancy, that's how the system worked and that fortune might take another idle sister out of the system and so on! So that same three hundred dollars earned hard running up and down the steps of high stoop houses in New York City could be the means of getting anything up to a dozen women under the blankets here in Ireland. And all pure legal!

There was no knowing the amount of people that'd get married at that time between Chalk Sunday and Shrove Tuesday. But quare times as the cat said when the clock fell on him, no one at all'd get married during Lent, or the rest of the year. So, if you weren't married by Shrove Tuesday night you could throw your hat at it. You'd have to wait another twelve months, unless you went out to Skelligs where the monks kept old time. Indeed a broadsheet used to come out called the Skelligs List; it used to be shoved under the doors Ash Wednesday morning. Oh, a scurrilous document in verse lampooning all those bachelors who should have, but didn't get married during Shrovetide.

From *In My Father's Time* by Eamon Kelly

THE WAY MATCHES WERE MADE ON CAPE CLEAR

I'll tell ye how I used to see the way in which matches were arranged. As you well know there is a season for everything, and Shrovetide is the season for matches. The young man, thinking of marrying would go to a spokesman and tell him to visit a particular house in search of a woman for him. The man of that house might have two or three daughters of marriageable age and just ripe for the taking. The spokesman and the young fellow then went off to him together. The spokesmen were glib talkers: if they weren't like that they wouldn't be any good at their job. When they reached the young woman's house the spokesman knocked on the door, and the man of the house would open the door and enquire: "What drove yourself on the road since 'tis rarely you visit us?" But, at the same time I suppose the man of the house half suspected what brought him. The spokesman would give the stick in his fist a shake and say: "I came seeking one of your daughters for this particular man." as he names the young fellow. "Come in and sit down 'till we have a talk a while," was the answer. After entering, the first thing the spokesman would do was to take out an old bottle he had in his pocket and give a glass out of the bottle to the man of the house in the hope that it might soften him. He then started to praise the youth to the very skies: his mode of life, his stock, his worldly substance, leaving not a single stone unturned so that he couldn't be refused. After the father had a brief conversation with his daughter it wouldn't take him long to give him a promise. The spokesman would then ask: "What dowry will you be able to give with this girl?" "I'll do my best; I'll give you the amount my means will allow me to give her." The bargain would be struck and the match made.

From *The Man From Cape Clear* by Conchúr Ó Síocháin

HASTE TO THE WEDDING

A century earlier the party would not have gone to the church at all. Instead, the priest would have come to the house and performed the ceremony there. In those days the wedding celebration was held in the house in which the young couple would live, which usually the young man's (or his parents') house, sometimes the bride's house, if the man was 'marrying in' there. In those days, too, the procession was from the bride's parents home to that of the bridegroom, in cars or carts, on foot, or - oftenest - on horseback with the women carried on pillions behind the men, with her father or elder brother carrying the bride. Often the young men raced furiously across country from one house to the other, and expected to be rewarded with bottles of liquor. Even when the church ceremony became usual this mad race was sometimes run from the house to the church and back again after the ceremony.

Arrived at the house about mid-morning, the party were bidden to fall upon the good things spread out. Often there was not room in the house for the throng, and tables were laid in the barn, or even in the farmyard. Often too, if it was known that a very large crowd would gather, tactful neighbors had helped things on with presents of fowl, bacon, bread, cakes and beverages, for any appearance of shortage or niggardliness at a wedding was a source of shame for all concerned, and might be 'thrown up against them' by some ill-intentioned person at a fair or a market years afterwards.

Usually the merrymaking was directed by a friend of the groom, acting as a sort of master of ceremonies. He marshalled the musicians and kept them suitably lubricated, and called for the next song or dance as occasion arose. The fun was well under way by the time the priest arrived. It was demanded by custom that the priest should stay on at the party after the marriage, and so his other parish duties for the day must have been already performed. Needless to say the parish clerk was in attendance, full of importance, and to all outward appearances seeming much more concerned with the proper order of things than the pastor himself. On the priest's coming all music and noise was stilled, and the guests crowded into the kitchen to see the couple joined. The ceremony over, the priest called for witnesses, and many pressed forward to have the honour of being recorded by name.

Then the priest was given a place of honour; if he were known to be a singer or musician, he was at a later stage requested by the groom or one of the older people to entertain the company with a song or tune.

From *In Ireland Long Ago* by Kevin Danaher

MARRIAGE CUSTOMS

FROM AN IRISH FOLKLORE
COMMISSION MANUSCRIPT

Long ago people used to get married different to the present time. There were a lot of runaway marriages. The man used to steal the girl to a neighbor's house a week before the marriage, then he and she would go on horseback to the church, and a boy and a girl they would choose themselves would stand sponsor for them.

When a boy would intend to marry a girl, and another boy would take plenty of whiskey and when they would have plenty of courage, they would take a quart bottle of whiskey to the house, and when they would have the father merry, they would ask him for the daughter. When they would be getting married, they would bring a married woman to church with them, they would get married on a Wednesday, because it was the luckiest day to get married. Friday and Saturday are the unlucky days to get married.

When the married couple would be leaving the church, somebody would throw an old shoe over the bride's head so that she would have good luck. The man used to give the bride gold, and she should buy something that would last for a long time, such as furniture.

If they did not meet a man on the way home they would have bad luck. They would not go to Mass until the second Sunday and if their sponsors were not with them on the second Sunday they would not go. The first Sunday they would go to Mass was called *Eirigh Amach*. When they would be going home after getting married, the bride's mother-in-law, if she had any, should break the wedding cake on her head when she would be coming in the door, then she would be friendly with her while she lived. If she had no mother-in-law, the married pair should cut the wedding cake and give a bit to everyone in the house. If anyone put a piece of it under their head for three nights, they would dream of their future wife or husband. If they spoke at all from once they went to bed, they would not dream at all. They should take the longest road home from the church. If they walked to the church they would have no luck.

The night of the wedding, the married couple should dance first. The neighboring boys used to dress up as straw, and go to the wedding house; they used to get a big, long pole and tie a note on the top of it with the words, "send out a drink." They would put the top of the pole in the door first. Drink was very cheap at that time and the married man would send out a bottle. When they would have it taken, they would come in and dance.

From the 1938 manuscripts of the
Irish Folklore Commission

It's why women marry - the creatures,
God bless them, are too shy to say no.

A young man is bothered until he is
married. After that he's bothered entirely.

It's a lonesome washing that there's not a man's shirt in it.

O woman if you join my strong clan
Your head will hold a golden crown.
Fresh killed pork, new milk and beer,
We shall share, O Lady Fair.

Blessing for a young man contemplating marriage:
That you might have nicer legs than your own under your table
before the new spuds are up.

At one time, single and newly married women would make a ball by
braiding and interlacing hair from horses or cows.
The ball was then presented as a token of affection
to the loved one.

It was customary to serve pancakes on
Shrove Tuesday. The eldest girl in a family would toss the first pancake.
If she did it perfectly she would make a good match.
If not, marriage was not in her future for the next year.

An Irish mother would sometimes remove her wedding ring and
put it in the pancake mixture. When the pancakes were served,
the person getting the ring would be lucky in marriage.
They also had to return the ring, of course!

Of all the stages in a woman's life, none is so dangerous
as the period between her acknowledgement of a passion for
a man, and the day set apart for her nuptials.
HUGH KELLY - *Memoirs of a Magdalen*

Whatever joys await the blest above,
no bliss below like happy wedded love.
WILLIAM ALLINGHAM

THE STRAWBOYS AT THE WEDDING

We had entered the countryside which was still steeped in the old traditions and customs, closely followed, although their origins were often lost. The young people could not say why they danced on the great slabs covering the dolmens - those tombs of kings who lived, perhaps, four thousand years ago when the Megalithic culture of the Mediterranean countries existed also in Ireland - but dance there they did, each Midsummer's Eve, having brought with them offerings of flowers. For aeons, these dolmens were centers of fertility rites, perhaps because of some dim but universal belief that where death and decay had been, birth and growth might spring.

So on an April day Nancy and Frank got married, and the Strawboys came and danced at their wedding. "What did they look like?" I asked, when a week later I made up the long borheen to see the bride. "They had high caps on them made of straw, pointed-like," said Nancy. "And masks, and straw capes round their shoulders. They'd straw tied up in front of their legs as well. They came at sundown - about eight o'clock, new time - and stayed half an hour. They danced with all but never spoke." "If they spoke t'would break the spell," the bridegroom interjected. "They take no refreshment either." " "And it's to bring good luck?" I asked. "'Tis," Nancy said, as a long intimate look passed between husband and wife, and I thought of the ancient fertility rites, which always seemed near and credible in the countryside. "Do you know where the Strawboys come from?" I asked. "Somewhere back in the hills," Nancy said. "But Frank thought a couple of them might have been comrades of his. "'Tis years and years since the Strawboys were seen in these parts, and there was a great cheer when we seen them coming, high up across the crags, just as the sun went down."

From a booklet by Luba Kaftannikoff, sent to Padraic Colum and included in his book, *Treasury of Irish Folklore*

JACK MULLOWNEY'S POTTTHALOWNG

This is an old saying that means an awkward, unfortunate
mishap that's not very serious, but comes just at the wrong time.

'Jack had gone to spend a pleasant evening at the home of his
future bride. He wore his best clothes: body coat, white waistcoat,
caroline hat (tall silk hat) and ducks (snow-white canvas trousers).
All sat down to a grand dinner given in his honour,
the young couple, side by side. Jack's plate was heaped up with
beautiful bacon and turkey, and white cabbage swimming in
fat that would make you lick your lips to look at it. Poor Jack was a bit
sheepish, for there was a good deal of banter. He drew over his plate to
the very edge of the table and in trying to manage a turkey bone with
knife and fork, he turned the plate right over into his lap,
down on the ducks.
The marriage came off all the same, but the story went
round the country like wildfire and for many a long day,
Jack had to stand the jokes of his friends on the potthalowng.'

3

FROM ATTIRE TO TRANSPORTATION

Since ancient times and until this century, an Irish bride wore her best dress to the wedding. Or, if the budget would allow it, she'd have the village 'nanty' make one for her. For hundreds of years, blue was a favorite color and silk the preferred fabric. Even though it had been introduced hundreds of years ago by a Celt, Anne of Brittany in 1499, the all-white wedding gown didn't come into popular vogue until quite recently. Isolated for many years from the whims of fashion, Irish brides followed the traditions of world-wide custom and wore whatever represented the best they had, embellished by jewelry, embroidery and lace. 'Shingerleens,' they were called - those small bits of finery, ornamental tags and ends of ribbons, bow knots, tassels and other adornments that could transform a best dress into a vision even the fairies might envy.

Envious, too, they would be of a typical sixteenth-century groom in his bright yellow silk shirt. Pleated in all directions from shoulder to wrist and neck to waist, its incredible color was captured from a dye made with Autumn crocuses. On top, he might have worn a short jacket made of the softest linen. Often embellished with intricate embroidery, the sleeves were left open along the underside so that the pleats of the shirt could flow down. Completing the ensemble would have been a pair of tight-fitting breeches and a sleeveless cloak, clasped at the shoulder with a brooch. From all perspectives, he would have cut a dashing figure. True to his ancestors and just as true in thought, word, and deed to the woman he was about to marry, the groom of long ago carried his cloak with pride and rode on horseback to meet her.

In this section, I have attempted to put an Irish slant on many of the details that must be taken care of before the ceremony - from attire to transportation. To facilitate finding each element, they're arranged in alphabetical order. While there's an old Irish proverb which says 'neither make nor break a custom,' the intention is to recognize our heritage in ways that are appropriate, but with the understanding that many of the old traditions would be considered out of place today - a bridal cloak of brilliant red, for example. According to eleventh-century legend, Mourne O'Glanny made such a garment for her wedding to Aran Roe. Thus, with a nod to our ancient ancestors combined with an acknowledgement that we live in the 21st century, I hope you will view all of the following ideas simply as suggestions.

I also urge the use of a month-by-month wedding planner. Most of the bridal magazines include one in every issue and it will be invaluable in organizing every element. Note too, that certain details you may want appear in other chapters. You will find suggestions for the programs under 'Ceremony' and ideas for table favors under

Long ago, Irish brides would never have worn a green wedding gown. It was thought to be a temptation to the fairies to steal the bride away.

It's good luck to have your birthstone in your engagement ring, even if that stone is otherwise thought to be an unlucky gem.

The earrings you wear on your wedding day will bring you luck and happiness ever after.

It's considered lucky to accidentally tear your bridal gown on your wedding day.

It's good luck if a married woman puts the veil on you, but bad luck to put it on yourself.

If you look at the sun when you leave for your wedding, your children will be beautiful.

'Reception.' Ultimately, regardless of what you wear, your decor, or any other aspect, what every couple should hope to achieve on the big day is an occasion of joy and merriment - of itself, a tradition as old as the land of our fathers.

ATTIRE

BRIDE

BRIDAL GOWN

While I love the dress our daughter chose, I did have her try on a gown similar to the one the bride wore in *The Quiet Man* - long sleeves, high neckline - very modest. It reminded me of the stories my mother told me about her wedding dress which she described as being made of Irish lace. On her head, she wore a Spanish-style mantilla and with her long black hair, pale complexion and grey-blue eyes, she must have looked stunning. I wish there was a photo I could share with you, but, as with many immigrants, old family albums were left behind and lost. I can tell you though, that my mother followed all the traditions of Ireland and the Roman Catholic Church and, while today's rules have been greatly relaxed, if you have any doubts, either opt for a gown like my mother's, or ask your celebrant well before you begin trying on dresses.

You might also, if you live in New York City, consult with Peggy and Martin Lacey. She is from County Galway and he is from County Kildare. Together, they own Saymel's Bridal Salon, reputedly the most popular bridal boutique in the Irish community. Many of their customers plan to marry at home in Ireland, so they particularly appreciate having an Irish opinion when choosing an appropriate

---

In ancient times, brides used herbs and not flowers in their bouquet because it was thought they had the power to ward off evil spirits. Some herbs had specific meanings as well: if a bride carried sage (the herb of wisdom), she would become wise; if she carried dill (the herb of lust), she would be lusty; and, if she carried rosemary, she would be endowed with the power of remembrance.

gown. Current trends, according to Peggy, indicate that many of their customers are selecting off-white because it suits the Irish complexion. Customers also appear to prefer understated, graceful lines and elegant, simple styles. "Puffs," says Peggy, "are out." What is definitely in is Celtic braiding, a look made popular by Irish-based designers, Sharon Hoey and Kathy De Stafford. Irish-born Mary Gristwood of Celtia Gowns in Scotland is also doing incredibly intricate embroidery, and the design team of Lorraine Gibbons and Miriam Spollen at Brontë Bridal Designs will astound you with their ability to carry through a Celtic motif, all the way from your gown to your train to your shoes.

Custom-made Gown

Perhaps the best way to incorporate authentic Irish detailing into your wedding dress is to have it made by a skilled seamstress. Alternatively, you could purchase a very simple gown and have it embellished with Irish white embroidery. Mountmellick work is probably the best known of this particularly beautiful embroidery style which features richly decorative patterns made with a thick cotton thread. There are manuals available that include full-size patterns which can be adapted to your needs. If you don't know a seamstress, and you live in a community that has an Irish dancing school, it may be useful to contact them and find out who is making their costumes. It may also be of value to check out *The Irish Dancer's Catalogue,* which features sew-it-yourself and embroider-it-yourself kits and, if you have access

My gown was a bit different from the typical, puffy white dress. It was ivory with white gold embroidered stitching making beautiful swirls on the skirt, almost like soft Celtic flower designs. My husband, being nostalgic for that sort of thing, wore something similar to what his father wore on his wedding day - black tuxedo pants with an ivory shirt and jacket. We added green and gold vests for some excitement.
It looked really sharp.

CONTRIBUTED BY
KATE MCLAUGHLIN

to the internet, there are several web pages which could be helpful. Interestingly, what I found out in my research, is that the designs embroidered on Irish dancing costumes traditionally come from The Book of Kells.

Should you decide that you would like to incorporate Celtic embroidery into your gown, the following advice from JoAnn Buck, who is a skilled seamstress and expert embroiderer, should prove to be very helpful:

- Select the design before you select the dress or at least the approximate size of the design. Your nearest bookstore should have a stock of Dover Publications. They publish a number of Celtic design books.
- Select the dress with the design in mind:
  1) areas to be embroidered should not be too "structured" and have very little or no lining and stiffening.
  2) some materials are more "embroiderable" than others. You may want to find your embroiderer first and ask for advice. Check with local needle craft shops or the local chapter of the Embroiderer's Guild for the names of embroiderers in your area. Ask to see examples of their work and don't use people who are hesitant about doing this type of embroidery.
  3) if the dress needs alterations have them done *before* it is embroidered.
  4) ask the embroiderer if an embroidery hoop will be used. Some fabrics may get stretched out of shape or the hoop could leave marks.
  5) suggestions for areas to be embroidered: hems and end of sleeves - especially if they come to a point. That is the perfect place for a small Celtic knot and it looks great on the "cut the cake" photos!
  6) always remember - less is more! White on white is preferable to a dark color on white. Very pale pastel embroidery also works well.

Another way to incorporate Irish craftsmanship into a custom-made gown is with embroidered net lace. Carrickmacross is the most famous and was created by Mrs. Grey Porter of

Carrickmacross, County Monaghan in 1816. During her honeymoon in Europe, she was so inspired by Italian appliqué lace that when she returned home, she began adapting it and ended up creating her own individual style. Eventually, she established a lace-making school and started a cottage industry which was of great assistance to the local economy. There are books available which explain the stitches and procedures and include full-size patterns; there is also at least one manual available on Limerick Lace which includes a section on how to make it, the materials required, designs, embroidery stitches and more.

BRIDAL HEADPIECE AND VEIL

The best advice I can give every bride-to-be is *not* to choose your headpiece or veil on the same day you select your gown. Allow some time to elapse before you make a final decision. In all of the excitement of finding *the* dress, it's too easy to make the wrong choice. You'll be much more objective if you wait a while. Also, think twice about choosing the headpiece or veil that a manufacturer has created to match your gown. Too often, it won't flatter your face shape or go with your hairstyle. A better alternative is to take your gown to a boutique that specializes in bridal veils. While wearing your dress, you'll be able to try various combinations of headpieces and veiling until you find a style that is exactly right for you.

In the absence of a wedding veil specialist in your community, your next best alternative is to have a photograph taken of yourself in the gown and send it to an excellent resource such as Paris Hats & Veils in Cincinnati, Ohio. They have created veils and headpieces for brides all over the world, are very pleasant to work with and surprisingly inexpensive. Another possible resource is Colleen Collections, a company located in County Galway that creates handcrafted Irish wedding tiaras. They ship to the United States and the price not only includes shipping and import duty, but also a complimentary good luck horseshoe made especially to coordinate with the style and color of the tiara.

Perhaps the biggest advantage of using a bridal veil specialist is that you can discuss with them how they might be able to incorporate Irish details on the headpiece. Or perhaps they could create a mantilla-style veil made from an Irish lace accessory. I did find another American company that specializes in customized tiaras and veils; Bridal Creations in Plainville, Connecticut will design and make exactly what you want - and they promise to do it less expensively than anyone else. Of course, if you are having your gown custom-made, then your seamstress will most likely be capable of creating the veil and headpiece as well. The most important thing to remember is selecting a style that suits you. You should also make certain that whatever veil and headpiece you choose, it's made so that the veil is detachable. You'll really appreciate the convenience at your reception.

WEDDING CLOAK

For a very old-fashioned and delightfully authentic Irish look, you might consider completing your ensemble with a classic Bridal Cloak and detachable hood. Siobhanwear is a company in County Cork that designs and hand-crafts these charming garments in 100% bainin worsted wool or a combination of light-weight bainin wool and Irish linen. Both are fully lined with off-white crinkle silk. The company ships overseas and they do have a toll-free telephone number as well as a web site.

IRISH WEDDING COORDINATORS

These days, many couples are putting all of the myriad details of planning the perfect wedding into the hands of a professional coordinator. If your budget allows it, I highly recommend that you make use of this service, because it gives you the luxury of relaxation and tranquility at a time when you need it most! If you need assistance beyond the suggestions in this book, I recommend that you contact one of the coordinators in the resource listing. Three of them are in Ireland and one is in the United States.

BRIDESMAIDS

You'll be more in keeping with Irish weddings as they used to be if you decide not to ask your bridesmaids to spend a fortune on dresses that they may wear only once. In fact, it's becoming quite popular for bridesmaids to select a dress that flatters their individual shape, so, while everyone is wearing shades of the same color, the styles may be completely different. When was the last time you were asked to be a bridesmaid and the bride said you could simply wear your best outfit? Unheard of? Different? Most definitely affordable! Should you prefer however, to stay within the realms of contemporary tradition, you can incorporate an Irish flair into the bridesmaid's dresses in the same ways already described for the bridal gown. What is also refreshingly different about today's styles is that we're no longer confined to those unattractive taffeta concoctions of years ago. Nowadays, a bridesmaid's dress can be very sophisticated and elegant and many of the most popular colors, including gold and champagne will work well in an Irish color scheme. Consider too, in your choice of gowns for the wedding party, details that are symbolic of old Ireland - cloaks and shawls for example. In our daughter's case, the gown she selected for her bridesmaids came with a long stole. We draped it over one shoulder and pinned it to the gown with a large Tara-style brooch.

FLOWER GIRL

Simple is best and definitely more appropriate than many of the dresses I've seen which resemble miniature bridal gowns. A charming outfit would be an old-fashioned white pinafore topping a solid color dress. Also keep in mind that while little girls wearing hats or halos of flowers look lovely, they can be uncomfortable. Often, a very young flower girl will remove her hat or other headpiece just at the wrong moment. Better to avoid this situation by allowing your flower girl(s) to have their hair arranged in the usual way, but perhaps with the addition of ribbons that coordinate with their dresses. This would be in keeping with how young Irish girls adorned their hair in the seventeenth century. An English judge who lived in County Limerick wrote an account of life in Ireland in 1620 and mentions that unmarried girls decorated their braided hair with yards of colored ribbon.

GROOM & GROOMSMEN

Medieval-style weddings are enjoying a resurgence of popularity and the costumes once worn by men during those times tie in well to a Celtic celebration. Earlier in this chapter, I described what a typical sixteenth-century bridegroom might have worn. Going back much further in history, Irish men of the nobility wore long tunics that reached halfway down the shin and a sleeveless, knee-length cloak which could be worn loosely or wrapped tight and fastened with a large brooch. Active young men such as soldiers and hunters generally wore a short jacket and tightly fitted trousers, sometimes fastened at or below the knee with buttons.

Often, men's tunics and women's dresses were made of white linen that was embroidered or appliquéd in gold or a bright color such as red, blue, purple or yellow. Patterned materials were also widely used and cloaks in particular were adorned with borders, stripes and fringes. Our ancestors also wore shoes and sandals that were dyed or decorated. These were saved for special occasions since the old literature indicates that both kings and peasants preferred to go barefoot.

Planning a much more modern celebration? The groom and the groomsmen will look very dashing if their tuxedo accessories, including vests, cummerbunds, cravats or bowties, match or compliment the bridesmaid's dresses. Alternatively, for a very informal wedding, you could consider a look that has long been popular in Ireland - grandfather shirts topped with a sleeveless waistcoat and slacks.

Yearning to see the men of the wedding party in kilts? There has been a great deal of debate on whether or not the ancient Irish wore them. Some scholars insist they did, and indeed, an illustration from the Book of Kells shows a man wearing what looks very much like a short, pleated garment. So, if you have your heart set on this look, go for it. In fact, each county in Ireland now has its own "tartan" and there's even a predominantly blue St. Patrick's tartan. There are also tartans available for Irish surnames. But a word of caution: These are modern day inventions, and while a pleated garment may have been worn in the old days, this author can find no historic basis for either the family or county patterns on offer. It may help to understand that a tartan represents, by line and color, historic events in the history of the family. So, perhaps it would be best to always refer to these new patterns as plaids - not tartans.

RING BEARER

I've yet to find a reference to the role of ring bearer in Irish history. That doesn't mean it didn't exist but in the absence of any solid information, I would suggest that you keep the ring bearer's outfit simple. Fussy details, á la Little Lord Fauntleroy, may make him uncomfortable and fidgety. You might consider looking into the traditional costume of a male Irish dancer. I've seen some wonderfully handsome outfits consisting of black tunic-style jackets, knife-pleated solid-color kilts and knee-high socks.

SOMETHING OLD, SOMETHING NEW, SOMETHING BORROWED, SOMETHING BLUE

Something old

There's an old Irish superstition that a bride must walk down the aisle with a coin in her right shoe. This ensures that good

---

SHOE SHENANIGANS

One custom was for the bride to wear an old pair of shoes that had already been broken in. Maybe it was for comfort's sake, but I also heard that it was because of the old superstition about not tempting the 'good people' to steal a bride in brand new slippers. Another one was to hide the brides shoe's while everyone was enjoying the feast so she could not run away on the wedding night. The other tradition I remember was to tie a few old ones to the rear bumper of the bride and groom's car. I believe that they still do that in Ireland nowadays.

When I asked one of my uncles what made a good wife, he looked very thoughtful and then said quite seriously, "You have to look for a big strong woman that could pull the plough if the horse gets tired!" The average age of marriage for women when I was growing up was 28 to 30 and for men at least 42. Men were not considered "finished" until they were 40. Marriage was a VERY serious thing.

CONTRIBUTED BY NORA WHO IS ORIGINALLY FROM IRELAND
AND NOW LIVES IN THE USA.

fortune will smile on the marriage. So, for something old, try to find a small pre-euro Irish coin or purchase one that comes 'ready to wear' in its own little satin sack. Most Irish shops and catalogs carry this very popular item. Alternatively, it was customary for the bride to wear an old piece of heirloom jewelry to symbolize the joy and love she brings to her future home.

While it's considered unlucky for a bride to cry before her wedding, tears of joy are often shed after the vows have been exchanged. To prepare for this probability, yet another charming something old is carrying an heirloom family handkerchief. In the old days, long before the invention of tissues, both men and women carried hankies; for the ladies, these were often very fancy and would be chosen to match an ensemble. This is an idea I found long after the first edition of this book was published. It would have been a lovely gesture for our daughter to carry one of the handkerchiefs that belonged to her great-grandmother as we inherited dozens of them. To enhance the link with the past, my source for this idea suggests tieing a bit of rosemary into one corner. This fragrant herb symbolizes remembrance and will remind the bride of the relative who carried the hanky before.

Today, a handkerchief is often presented to the mothers of the groom and the bride at the beginning of the service to honor and thank them. Not surprisingly, this charming token is often put to use immediately. Don't have an heirloom hanky in the family? Not to worry - see 'Something new' for a great alternative.

Something new

This is usually the wedding dress or new accessory bought especially for the wedding. It signifies the new life the bride is embracing and the success she wishes on her husband and married life. While most brides opt for their wedding gown as the something new, why not be more original and make it a magic hanky? A lovely old Irish custom, the magic hanky is carried on the wedding day and then put away until the christening of the first child. With a few cleverly placed stitches, it is then turned into a christening bonnet. After the christening, it is put away again until the child grows up and marries. On that wedding day, a few snips will turn it back into a hanky. By then, it will make for a most appropriate 'something old.'

You'll find magic hankys made of pure Irish linen and lace in Irish specialty stores, at Celtic festivals, and in catalogs.

Something borrowed

In Ireland, it's said that if the bride borrows something from a happily married woman, then her marriage will be happy, too. It also signifies the bride's wish to bring a part of her old life with her. On my wedding day, instead of a bouquet, I carried a white Roman Catholic missal decorated with white ribbons and roses. It was a gift from my husband's parents. Until recently, it sat in a drawer, carefully wrapped - and long forgotten. One evening, our daughter and I were both lamenting that somehow in numerous moves, my wedding gown and veil had disappeared and I had nothing tangible from my big day to pass on to her. Then I remembered the missal. Our daughter was thrilled to 'borrow' it and had it decorated in much the same way that I did. Alternatively, you might ask a relative or friend if you can borrow a piece of jewelry or perhaps a pair of gloves, if they would be appropriate with your gown. The important thing to remember is that whatever you borrow, it's lent to you by someone who is happily married.

Something blue

Irish brides once considered blue to be very lucky; it is also the color of fidelity, love and purity, and symbolizes a bride's commitment to her husband. If your color scheme includes blue, you might consider blue Celtic braiding sewn into the bodice of your wedding gown. You could also wear a blue slip (but be sure it doesn't show through), or perhaps a garter trimmed in blue ribbon. These are readily available in most wedding invitation catalogs. Other ideas for something blue is to carry a blue handkerchief, incorporate a blue ribbon into your bouquet, or perhaps the easiest and most fun one of all that I recently heard about - paint your toenails blue!

COLOR SCHEME

While green immediately springs to mind when most people think of Ireland, it may come as a surprise to learn that it didn't become the country's official color until the 19th century. Prior to that, and for hundreds of years, Ireland's national color was St. Patrick's blue. In fact, at one time, her flag featured a gold harp on a blue background. That was later replaced by a green background and this in turn was changed to the present day tricolor banner of the Republic. So, if you should be inclined to honor your heritage by selecting a blue and gold color scheme, you would be using hues that have a much longer cultural history than any one of Ireland's forty shades of green.

There are many other color options worth investigating. Pink, for example, appears to be an extremely popular house color in many of the places we visited, especially in the coastal towns of Kinsale and Kenmare. Other pastels too, from pale yellow to light blue are also very much a part of the scenery. Combined with hanging baskets and window boxes cascading with blooms, the effect is both charming and delightful. Out in the countryside, distant mountains look purple, at least one range of cliffs takes on a lavender hue in a certain light, and everywhere, the moors and hills are sprinkled with heather and wildflowers. So don't limit your choice to green - become inspired as our ancestors did and perhaps create a color scheme reminiscent of an Irish landscape.

An attractive way to weave Irish colors into your wedding attire and decor is to use your family crests. Hundreds of Irish names and clans claim a special crest emblematic of their lineage. Many of these feature wonderful color combinations that would be very appropriate, especially if both of you are Irish. You could perhaps,

Most couples are aware of the rule that the groom cannot see the bride in her gown before the wedding day. It was also the rule that the bride should not see her entire reflection in the mirror. If she sees herself in her full regalia, it is thought that part of her will remain in her old life and not move on with the rest of her. If either of these rules was broken, the wedding was usually put off for a year.

take one color from each crest and combine the two in a symbolic tribute to the uniting of your families.

If you're to be married in the fall, the Republic's national colors of green, white and orange would make for an appropriately seasonal combination. The red skirts worn for centuries by women in the Aran Isles also offer inspiration, especially if you're planning to be married in winter or during the Christmas season, and particularly if your family has roots in the west of Ireland.

Ireland's 'soft weather' - the euphemism often used to describe a misty rain - could inspire a color scheme based on various shades of gray. An Irish sky is remarkably varied and seems to change constantly. Dark, glowery clouds frequently give way to brilliant shafts of sunlight which cast a magical, almost luminous light on the land.

So, while green is, indeed, inexorably linked to the Emerald Isle, it's not the only color that could perfectly express your Irish heritage. Be creative, and consider other options reflective of Ireland's rich color palette as well as your own very personal taste.

FLOWERS

Be sure to tell your florist that you are planning an Irish wedding. Mention the many flowers that grow profusely in Ireland's mild climate, including foxglove, roses, rhododendrons, and yes, even orchids. In coastal towns such as Glengariff and Bantry, there are stunning subtropical gardens and even in Galway, we were surprised to see palm trees thriving. A good floral designer will be happy to suggest combinations based on swatches of the materials your are using for the bridal party. Our own florist combined roses, bells of Ireland, eucalyptus, trailing ivy and other flowers to create bouquets, arrangements, flower baskets, corsages and boutonniéres. All of the flowers she used are readily available in the United States, yet captured the romantic Celtic aura we desired. Below are some suggestions that may be helpful in choosing your flowers. Note that ideas for the ceremony and reception will be found within those chapters.

FLORAL HEADPIECE

According to the history books, it was during medieval times that brides began wearing wreaths of real flowers in their hair - a lovely old custom that would be just as appropriate for today's bride and her attendants.

FLOWERS AND THEIR MEANING

In my entire life, I don't think I've met anyone who knew so many superstitions as my Dublin-born mother. We couldn't cut our nails on Sunday, or wash our hair; an itchy right hand meant money; putting new shoes on a table was bad luck and a bed could never face the door! She was also superstitious about flowers. It was bad luck, for example to bring lilac or apple blossoms into the house. And she attached meanings to flowers that appear to be universal: ivy means faithfulness, roses always communicate love, laurel means peace, lilies mean purity, shamrock means loyalty, and Bells of Ireland are lucky, as are heather and myrtle. In fact, brides in Wales once carried live myrtle in their bouquets. After the wedding, they would give a sprig to their unmarried bridesmaid(s). It would then be planted and if it grew, the bridesmaid would be married within the year.

*No match or race or
dance there's been
Where throngs assemble on the green,
At which I've let myself be seen
Except well-dressed, from head to foot,
In clothes all chosen well to suit,
Just enough powder on my head,
On which a well-starched
coif I spread,
And over that a hood of white
Graced with a set of ribbons bright.
The printed frock I wear I deck
With ruffs both at the wrist and neck
My scarlet cloak you'll rarely view
Without some aery facing new.
A faery queen might envy me
This linen apron which, you see,
Is covered with embroidery
Of plant and herb and bird and tree.
I'd sharp stiletto heels with screws
To lift the insteps of my shoes.
Buckles, silk gloves and rings add
grace
To hoops and bracelets and old lace.*

BRIAN MERRIMAN

Green Carnations

While they always remind me of St. Patrick's Day parades, if they go with your color scheme, by all means incorporate them into your floral decor if that's what you would like - but a word of caution - my mother would have shaken her head in dismay because carnations meant a funeral!

Shamrocks

The plant grown in America and other countries is called Oxalis and has a much larger leaf than the one native to Ireland. However, if your wedding will take place during the month of March, you may wish to consider incorporating genuine imported shamrock into bouquets, corsages and boutonnières. Ask your florist to check into availability.

Irish Flowers

If you'd like to use only those flowers that grow in Ireland, a good resource is a book by D.A. Webb called *Irish Flora*. Except for the rare species of wild flowers that are found in places like the Burren, most of the flowers cultivated in Ireland today are also grown in the USA and other countries.

Whatever you decide to use for your floral decor, you'll be more in step with Irish tradition if you choose fresh blooms in season - as long as you leave those unlucky lilacs and apple blossoms to bloom where they're planted! Also, be sure to avoid yellow flowers which mean jealousy and tulips which mean infidelity.

INVITATIONS

Finding the perfect invitation has become much simpler since the Lantz at Killary line of wedding stationery was introduced. Irish-owned and Dublin-based, Lantz was established in 1976 and has become one of the country's leading manufacturers and suppliers of wedding stationery. After seeing just a few of their spectacular samples I can see why. And I can almost guarantee that most couples will find what they're looking for. Included in the line are Celtic themes inspired by historic and religious images and by myths, legends, and traditional jewelry. One of the themes is taken from the spirals at Newgrange, an ancient burial site on the River Boyne in County Meath. Some of the artifacts taken from the chamber have been carbon dated to between 2675 and 2485 BC which makes the site even older than the pyramids in Egypt.

Another Celtic theme is inspired by the Tara brooch which was originally made during the Bronze Age. Also represented in the line is the immensely popular Claddagh symbol. (For the legend of the Claddagh, look under Jewelry later in this chapter) And for those seeking a regal touch, the family crest of more than 400 Irish names can be incorporated into two particular designs. The company also offers a wide range of both contemporary and traditional invitations as well as a broad offering of related products, including thank you cards, program covers, envelope seals and cake boxes. Another Irish stationer who recently came to my attention is Historical Irish Wedding Stationery in County Clare. Their web site shows some lovely designs, and for a small fee, they will send you a catalog.

Logically, the catalogs advertised in bridal magazines are a good place to begin looking for appropriate stationery designs. However, I have not found any recent catalogs that offer invitations featuring Irish or Celtic-inspired motifs. I wasn't looking for them, but to save you the trouble if you are, I also didn't find any designs with shamrocks or leprechauns!

CUSTOM DESIGNED INVITATIONS

Undoubtedly, the most personal invitation is one designed by the bride and groom. If the budget permits, check into commissioning a Celtic artist or, if you have artistic skills, apply them to creating what will become a memorable keepsake. Illumination would be lovely, as would a design that incorporates your family crest. Your own version of the Claddagh symbol would also be very appropriate as would a Celtic cross, knot or mandala. Once you have your design complete, it's then a simple matter of contacting a reputable printer who will reproduce it on whatever wedding stationery components you desire. The printer can also reproduce your wording in just about any typeface, but if you really want a Celtic look, you may need to hire a calligrapher. Most metropolitan areas will have local calligraphers listed in the telephone book. Alternatively, you might consider utilizing one of several Celtic alphabets illustrated in a clip-art book by Mallory Pearce. Also available by Pearce is a book featuring easy-to-duplicate (and copyright-free) Celtic borders. For those of us not blessed with artistic talent, yet determined to create something unique, these are invaluable!

INVITATION WORDING

The tradition in Ireland is to have the word 'Invitation' or 'Wedding Invitation' on the outside of what is called the day invitation (to distinguish it from an evening invitation which is commonly used to invite friends and acquaintances not actually attending the wedding reception, but whom the happy couple wish to be part of the celebrations).

The wording on the inside of the day invitation is also different. Instead of saying you're going to be married to someone, the Irish say married with someone, For example:

Mr. and Mrs. Scott Haggerty
request the honour of your presence
at the marriage of their daughter
Helena Bridget
with
Terence Brendon O'Flaherty.
Saturday, the fifth of October
in the year two thousand
at two o'clock
St. Joseph's Church
Skibbereen, County Cork

It might sound strange to non-native ears, but apparently it's proper Irish etiquette. Ironically, it seems to me, 'with' implies a more equal partnership than the modern custom of 'to.' It should also be noted that in Ireland, it's customary for engagement announcements to list the order of birth in the family. So, if you were announcing your engagement in *The Irish Times* it would read as follows:

MR. BENJAMIN HAGGERTY
MISS RENEE SHIELDS
The engagement is announced between Renee
third daughter of Mr. and Mrs. Dennis Shields
Ballybitt, Rathvilly, County Carlow
and
Benjamin
second son of Mr. and Mrs. Charles Haggerty
8 Grattan Road, Galway City, County Galway.

SHAMROCK SEALING WAX

For an extra touch of old-fashioned Irish flair on your invitations, informals and thank you notes, use a wax seal on the envelopes. Many Irish stores and catalogs stock a set that includes a brass seal and two sticks of green wax.

ST PATRICK POSTMARK

For a real 'little bit of Ireland' you may like to know about a place called St. Patrick in Missouri. It was founded by Irish immigrants in 1833 and more than a hundred years later, one Fr. Francis O'Duignan, a young priest from County Longford, came to the tiny farming community. He dreamed of building a shrine to honor Ireland's patron saint and sent letters all over the world asking for donations. On each letter he put a shamrock cachet which he designed in 1936, stating: 'St. Patrick, Missouri, The Only One In The World.' He firmly believed that St. Patrick would bless all who aided in making the shrine possible. His dream was realized in 1957 when the Shrine of St. Patrick was dedicated on March 17. Fashioned after the Church of Four Masters in County Donegal, it includes Celtic crosses, a round bell tower and 37 stained glass windows made in Dublin.

Every St. Patrick's Day, the community puts on a big celebration with special church services and tours. While he can no longer attend the festivities for health reasons, County Mayo radio personality, Tommy Murphy, is still made Honorary Mayor for the day.

Well before the big day arrives, letters and cards come pouring in from all over the world to be mailed back out on March 17 sporting whatever the design is for the year and the traditional regulation postmark. Definitely a collector's item! For the past few years, the local post office has been authorized to use the special postmark for the entire month of March and it's not anticipated that this will change. That means that if it isn't absolutely essential to have the envelope cancelled on the 17th, you can still get the special design from the first of the month until the end of the month. And year-round, while the special design isn't available, you can most definitely get the customary black and white cancellation which says St. Patrick, Missouri.

POSTAGE

For several years, the United States Post Office has issued stamp designs that are appropriate for wedding invitations in general. Of all the designs, just one is symbolically Irish. A shamrock stamp exists in a group of nine others, each depicting a different holiday. So, you'd have to purchase a lot of stamps just to get the shamrock. Plus, you would also have to add a different stamp to make up the difference in postage. The impracticality of this approach led to a search for some other symbol that might be appropriate. In the first edition of this book, we had found a stamp depicting two swans kissing, their arched necks forming a heart. Since swans are a symbol of love because of their fidelity, and they're also a part of Irish legend, this one seemed ideal for an Irish wedding invitation. Unfortunately, we are told it has been discontinued. Here's one case where you'll have to put your Irish-inspired imagination to work and come up with an alternative!

Note: Before you mail your invitations, be sure to assemble one complete package and take it to the post office to be weighed. (Don't forget maps, if your guests will need them).

JEWELRY

Long ago, Irish royalty wore an abundance of fine gold ornaments, both men and women used Celtic brooches to fasten their cloaks, and in the Claddagh - a community across the Corrib river from Galway city - a tradition was born that has survived the Famine, the Troubles, and the distance that separates emigrants and their descendants from their homeland.

THE LEGEND OF THE CLADDAGH WEDDING RING

I've heard two stories about how the Claddagh originated. The first, lesser-known tale, says that Margaret Joyce married a wealthy Spanish merchant who traded with Galway. When he died, he left her a a great fortune. She returned to Galway and used her fortune to build bridges from Galway to Sligo. She was rewarded for her good works when an eagle dropped the original Claddagh ring into her lap.

The story that I like best however, and the one that's most familiar, says that in the sixteenth century, a fishing boat from the village of Claddagh was captured by Algerian pirates and the Irish crew, including a sailor named Richard Joyce, was sold into slavery. Richard, who was to be married the same week he was captured, was sold to a wealthy Moorish goldsmith who taught Richard the trade. Unable to forget his fiancé, Richard designed a ring for her of special significance: the hands meant friendship, the crown, loyalty, and the heart, love. Eventually Richard managed to escape and return to Ireland. When he arrived, he discovered that his girl had never married. They were wed and the ring he gave her was the one he had designed and made while he was a slave.

Over the years, the design became extremely popular as a betrothal or wedding ring and took on even more significance. Worn on the right hand with the heart pointing out means that the wearer's heart is uncommitted. Worn on the same hand with the heart pointing inward means that the wearer's heart is taken. Worn on the left hand with the heart pointing inward means 'Let Love and Friendship reign forever, never to be separated.' Claddagh rings were commonly worn by women on the west coast and off-shore islands, often representing the sole major investment of a fishing family, handed down from mother to daughter. Today, many couples, even those not of Irish descent, are choosing the Claddagh symbol for their engagement and wedding rings. They are widely available, as are a wide range of other Claddagh accessories from earrings and pendants to tie-tacs and cufflinks.

CRESTED RINGS

Heraldry began in Europe more than eight hundred and fifty years ago as a very necessary means of instant recognition to distinguish friend from foe on the battlefield. The symbols carried on armor and shields became objects of family pride borne on clothing and jewelry. Today, it's possible to trace and recreate in precious metals just about every Irish family crest and the coat-of-arms for each county.

GIMMEL OR BOND RING

Not as widely known as the Claddagh legend, this tradition goes back to the Middle Ages when solemn betrothal by means of the Gimmel or Bond Ring often preceded matrimony. Occasionally, it was adopted by lovers who were about to be separated for a long time. Comprised of three joined rings, it was customary to break the rings apart at the betrothal, which was ratified in a solemn manner over the Holy Bible and in the presence of a witness who was often a priest. The man and woman broke away the upper and lower rings from the central one, which the witness retained. When the couple was reunited, the three portions of the ring were once again joined together; it then took on the honor of becoming the bride's wedding ring.

LOVE LOCKETS AND HUMAN-HAIR BRACELETS

Long ago in Ireland, it was the custom for the man to give the woman he wanted to marry a bracelet woven of human hair - presumably his! Her acceptance of it was symbolic of accepting the man, linking herself to him for life. The use of strands of hair in love lockets, usually curled into a circle, is a custom that has been handed down to modern times. The circle of the bracelet, as in the wedding band and the round strand of hair, symbolize a union that will be linked together for all time.

CELTIC DESIGNS

During the past several years, there has been an amazing resurgence of interest in Celtic culture. Today, it's possible to purchase silver and enamelled brooches based on illumination from the seventh-century Book of Durrow, delicate bird motif earrings inspired by the ninth century Book of Kells, Celtic crosses of Irish crystal, and countless other creations that would add an authentic Irish touch to bridal party attire. If an Irish or Celtic Festival is held in your area, these offer great opportunities to see and examine first-hand the many stunning Celtic-inspired creations that are available today. Many Irish-related catalogs are also available which usually include significant sections devoted to jewelry.

OGHAM

Ogham is the ancient Irish alphabet and you might consider using it for engraving wedding bands and/or other pieces of jewelry engraved with your names, initials, wedding date or other meaningful inscription. Books containing the Ogham alphabet are available and Ogham accessories are available in several Irish catalogs.

CELETIC ALPHABET PENDANT

If you are looking for an unusual gift for the bridesmaids, consider a sterling silver pendant that features the initial of their first or last name. One design I've seen features capital letters taken from the *Book of Kells*.

TARA BROOCH

Our daughter gave each of her bridesmaid's a version of this national treasure which, as I've already mentioned, they used to fasten the stoles of their gowns. Centuries ago, both men and women of the wealthier classes would have worn a Tara or similarly-designed brooch, so consider it as part of the attire for all members of the wedding party.

EMERALDS

This is a natural choice for an Irish bride and groom and since the stone carries the meaning 'success', it bodes well for anyone who wears it.

These are just a few ideas that I hope will help in the selection of something more appropriate for an Irish bride to wear other than the usual string of pearls. And besides, according to another of my mother's superstitions, pearls bring tears - hardly propitious for what should be one of the happiest days in a woman's life!

LUCKY HORSESHOE

Irish brides once walked down the aisle carrying a real horseshoe. It was said that if she didn't, the couple would never have good fortune. The points of the horseshoe also had to be carried so the points were turned upward - 'so the luck wouldn't run out.' Nowadays, Irish brides still carry a horseshoe but it's more likely to be a small fabric one sewn into an inconspicuous part of the wedding gown. A small horseshoe might also be carried in the bride's bouquet. Yet another relatively modern idea is to wear a fabric horseshoe on the wrist.

My parents could not attend my wedding because they lived in London, England, and my father was too ill to travel. But they didn't let the day go by without making sure I carried a lucky horseshoe. On the wedding morning, a telegram arrived, accompanied by a very pretty silver horseshoe made of very heavy paper stock and decorated with white ribbons. The telegram of good wishes is also traditional and is sent to be read during the reception - which it was.

TRANSPORTATION

In the old days, a young couple walked to the church on their wedding day but since that isn't practical for most people, you could recognize Ireland's equestrian heritage by renting horses and carriages for the wedding party - or, at least, for the bride and groom. If you decide to do this, make your reservations early as it has become an extremely popular method of getting to and from the church and reception. Most carriage rental companies will decorate your carriage and the horses using the color scheme you give them. I have even heard of one company that had special horseshoes made with shamrocks carved in them! Make inquiries of several companies and visit their stables to make sure their horses are well taken care of. Reputable companies will welcome your visit. And while they will carry the required insurance for transporting people, keep in mind that you may need to take out extra insurance to cover guests and your reception venue. Depending on your budget, it may be more practical to stay with the traditional convoy of limousines. If that's what you decide to do, the bridal car can be decorated in contemporary Irish custom with white or off-white satin ribbons and bows.

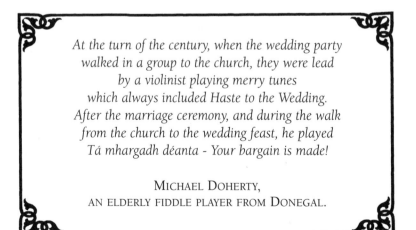

At the turn of the century, when the wedding party
walked in a group to the church, they were lead
by a violinist playing merry tunes
which always included Haste to the Wedding.
After the marriage ceremony, and during the walk
from the church to the wedding feast, he played
Tá mhargadh déanta - Your bargain is made!

MICHAEL DOHERTY,
AN ELDERLY FIDDLE PLAYER FROM DONEGAL.

Note: For companies, products or services mentioned in this chapter, please consult:
The Resource Listing in Section VI
The North American Celtic Buyers Association website.
If you live in the United States or Canada, they have a great search function that will enable you to find the nearest Irish shop:
www.celticbuyers.com
My website:
www.irishcultureandcustoms.com/Weddings/WeddingRsrcs.html

4

AITIN' THE GANDER
PRE-WEDDING PARTIES

Not so long ago, to hear the old storytellers tell about it, there used to be a custom that makes me wonder if today's term 'to cook one's goose' didn't have its origins in Ireland! When the matchmaker had succeeded in having the respective families of the bride and groom agree to a union, the groom was invited to come meet his future wife. It was on this occasion that the bride's family would roast a goose in honor of the up-coming nuptials. It was a chance for the couple to become better acquainted and all involved in the wedding would be invited, including the priest. Following dinner, there'd be dancing and plenty of opportunity for the couple to take a gander at what their families had lined up for them.

Another version of this same custom was called 'picking the gander.' It came by its name from when family members discussed the implications of married life with the blushing bride-to-be as they plucked or picked the feathers from the goose.

Following the 'Aitin of the Gander,' the families would get together to do 'The Bindings' - the marriage agreement. The agreement could often be extremely complicated. In many instances, for example, the daughter's mother and father would include a proviso that when they were old, they would get their full need of essentials such as milk, turf, butter, eggs and a ride to Sunday Mass.

In this chapter, you'll find menu suggestions and other ideas for Aitin' the Gander, hen parties, bridesmaid's luncheon or tea, stag parties and the rehearsal dinner.

If a dish is marked with an asterisk, you'll find the recipe in the recipe section and if it requires an Irish ingredient, you'll find where to buy it in the resource listing or on my website.

AINTIN' THE GANDER DINNER PARTY

I'd never cooked a goose before but it really wasn't any more difficult than preparing other poultry. I'd been warned about excessive grease but Darina Allen's recipe from her book, *Festive Foods of Ireland*, has a simple method for overcoming this problem. Since I was a little uncertain about the main course, I kept the rest of the menu very simple. It turned out well and the mashed potato stuffing has become a family favorite.

Entrée:	Michaelmas Goose with Potato Apple Stuffing* and Gravy*
Side-dish:	Chunky applesauce. Homemade is best, but if you don't have time to make your own, a store-bought mixture of apple and cranberry sauce goes well
Vegetable:	Green Cabbage, lightly steamed so it's still rich in color and not mushy
Accompaniment:	Blue Ribbon Feis Soda Bread* served with butter
Dessert:	Bunratty Apple Tart,* served with cream.

*A roast goose was traditionally served on the
feast of St. Michael, September 29. The first corn of the new year
was ground into flour and baked into bread
to go with the feast and the last sheaf of wheat
was the centerpiece on the table. In some parts of Ireland,
the girl who tied the wheat sheaf had the honor of being led
on the dance floor for the first dance of the evening.*

HEN PARTIES

An expression still commonly used to describe a shower given by friends of the bride, a hen party is customarily confined to just the womenfolk and the guest list usually includes the bride's mother, her future mother-in-law and other female relatives, as well as close friends. Often, it was - and still is - an occasion for bringing out the best china and linen upon which to spread a tempting array of dainty sandwiches, cakes, tarts, and other foods one associates with a formal high tea. As with most tea parties, the guest of honor is always the one who pours.

Traditionally, games are not played at an Irish hen party. But there is plenty of good conversation, excellent food and drink, and many oohs and aahs when the gifts are opened. While today's couples are often treated to several showers that include both men and women, there's something very special about the old-fashioned, all-female variety. The bride can open frilly lingerie without fear of embarrassment, the women of both families can gab to their heart's content, and it's a wonderful opportunity to show off one's culinary skills, especially if each guest brings a dish to share. Just about any finger sandwiches, cakes, tarts, and other sweets can make up the menu. Typically, it might include:

Cucumber sandwiches*
A tray of Irish cheeses and crackers
A tray of julienne vegetables and dip
Warm strawberry scones* served with whipped cream
Drop scones* served with butter and a variety of spreads
Profiteroles* (cream puffs) with Baileys Chocolate Sauce*
Irish Mist Cheesecake*
Sherry
Tea* - for the talkin'.

BRIDESMAID'S LUNCHEON

To show her gratitude for all the help and support she has been given prior to the wedding, it has become customary for the bride to give her bridesmaids a luncheon. If you live on the coast, near a lake, or close to a river, you could treat them to lunch at a restaurant with a water view, or, if there's one available, combine the meal with a cruise on a commercial riverboat. Ireland literally teems with lakes, river and streams and this could be a charming way to recognize a part of your heritage that quite likely will have a link to the water. It's also a poignant remembrance of immigrant ancestors who courageously traveled - many of them on crowded 'coffin ships' - to North America. If yours was one of them, this would be a wonderful way to toast their memory.

Alternatively, and especially if your budget can't afford a restaurant meal, consider a lunch in your home or apartment. If you have the luncheon on a weekend, you could rent a couple of Irish videos to watch afterwards. *The Quiet Man* would be a great choice. *Circle of Friends* and *The Matchmaker* are also excellent candidates. And, if any of your bridesmaids aren't of Irish extraction, this might be a great opportunity to introduce them to Irish culture by watching a video of *Riverdance* or Michael Flatley's *Lord of the Dance*. His *Feet of Flames* production is also now available on video. These shows are among the best stage spectaculars ever produced.

For a simple yet elegant, menu, consider:

Appetizer:	Oak-smoked salmon served on Irish Brown Bread*
Entrée:	Cold Chicken in Tarragon Sauce*
Vegetable:	New potatoes*
Salad:	Warm Spinach Salad*
Dessert:	Apple Snow* and Carolans Chip Cookies*

Λ SHOW OF PRESENTS

This is an old Irish custom where the bride invites female guests to her parent's home to see the wedding gifts set out. Customarily, after the viewing of the presents, the bride will serve a lunch or tea. The menus for either the Hen Party or the Bridesmaid's Luncheon would be appropriate for this event.

STAG PARTIES & BACHELORETTE PARTIES

If you live in a major metropolitan area, the chances are excellent that there are more than one or two Irish pubs where the men of the wedding party (and perhaps the women, too), could gather for the grooms's last 'hooley' before the wedding. All well and good, as long as there's a designated driver in the group who can make certain everyone arrives home safely. Alternatively, and more wisely, many stag groups are renting limousines for the evening so that all can indulge without worry. And while an Irish pub with sing-alongs, lively conversation, and maybe even a dart board or two would seem to be the most appropriate setting for a stag celebration, here are some other suggestions:

A Morning Golf Game
After the round, enjoy lunch at a bar that serves good pub grub.

'Walking the land' was the term used to describe an inspection of the future son-in-law's family home. It was conducted by the bride's parents and when it was over, they would then partake of the hospitality of the house to make certain there were no miserly tendencies in the young man's family.

Televised Sports Event and Ploughman's Lunch

There's usually a major soccer match or other sporting event taking place in any one season. With most people now having access to cable TV, this would provide exciting entertainment which could be followed by an impromptu game out in the back yard to work off the food. A typical menu for a home-fixed Ploughman's Lunch might include some or all of the following:

Sausage rolls*
Hard-boiled eggs with 'soldiers' (sliced bread toasted, buttered, and cut vertically into thirds)
Sharp Irish cheddar cheese and crusty bread
Irish country relish
Ham sandwiches
Dublin Potato Salad*
Plenty of stout!

An All-Day Fishing Trip

This could be followed by dinner at the best man's house. If the fish are biting, the main course could be the catch of the day, grilled on the barbecue. The big one got away? Salmon or trout are indigenous to Ireland and would be very appropriate substitutes. If the weather precludes a barbecue and/or the mariners come home empty-netted, a thoughtful best man might consider making a big pot of Irish Lamb Stew* ahead of time and reheating it when his wedding crew return from their angling adventure.

A Day at the Races

The Irish love their horses and they're particularly fond of the Sport of Kings. If there's a racetrack nearby, playing the ponies would be fun for both the men and women. End the day with a romantic dinner party at the best man's house and perhaps consider a menu somewhat more elegant than pub grub - perhaps a roast leg of lamb or a pork loin served with roast potatoes and baby peas. And for dessert, how about a Coffee and Walnut Gateau* filled and frosted with Baileys Coffee Icing.*

Handball

Organize a friendly tournament at a local sports facility. In Ireland, this game used to be played in backyards or against the gable-end of houses. It was brought to the United States by immigrants who played it in blind alleys, especially in cities on the East Coast. Always a fast and furious game, a few hours of this will call for a hearty meal - Irish Rarebit* or a traditional Irish Stew* made with Guinness and a side dish of Colcannon,* for example.

Road Bowling

If you live in a rural area where people in the road won't hinder traffic, then this could provide a grand diversion, but you'll need an iron ball, known as a 'bullet' which weighs 1lb. 10oz. You map out a course, and the winner is the player who needs the fewest throws to complete it. If the ball leaves the road, the player is penalized. (Perhaps he has to go back a few yards?). Playing around bends calls for great skill and the ability to put a spin on the 'bullet'. As with the previous idea, a few hours of boisterous road bowling is bound to work up a healthy appetite - and a thirst. You could visit your local tavern and partake of some stick-to-the-ribs food washed down with your favorite brew. Alternatively, the best man could have the lads over for a dish that was always served on Saturday nights, when the men came home from the pub. Directions for making Dublin Coddle appear in the recipe section.

Hurling

I would be remiss if I neglected to mention one of the oldest and most popular sports in Ireland, hurling. At one time, entire villages would compete with each other. The game would begin halfway between the villages. Equipped with sticks called hurleys, a team from one village would attempt to drive a small leather ball back to the main street of the opposing village. To adapt this game, you could find a recreation area with a public football field and play a modified version with hockey sticks and a softball. Divide the wedding party into two teams and choose one member from each team to serve as a goalkeeper. Points would be scored for successfully driving the ball under or over the cross bar of the goal posts. As with the previous physically strenuous ideas, this suggestion requires an ample supply of hearty food and liquid libation at game's end. Perhaps the winning team buys the first round of drinks?

THE REHEARSAL DINNER

Traditionally hosted by the groom's parents, the rehearsal dinner can vary considerably in degrees of formality. But whatever the venue, the most important suggestion I can make is that if your rehearsal is the evening before the wedding, as is customary in many countries, don't make a long night of it. With the big day just a few hours away, you want everyone to wake up feeling refreshed, energetic and certainly not with a hangover.

With that in mind, the groom's parents may wish to consider having a dinner comprised of an Irish menu catered at their home. To add to the festivities, perhaps a harpist could be hired to play during the meal. The rehearsal dinner and the reception are also when people will be called upon to make toasts. Generally a more intimate gathering than the reception, it's the perfect time to introduce what the Irish call 'slagging,' Similar to what is called 'roasting' in the United States and elsewhere, it usually involves good-natured kidding at the expense of the bridal couple and their families. A word of caution, though; the emphasis is on *good-natured* and if anyone has any doubts about a slagging remark, it should be avoided. As for menu ideas, here are three suggestions that range from a country style, old-fashioned Irish dinner to one that is more formal.

Irish Country Dinner
Entrée: Boiled Ham and Cabbage*
Vegetable: Potatoes boiled in their jackets
Accompaniment: Irish Brown Bread*
Dessert: Irish Apple Cake.*

Reminiscent of the Bunratty Banquet
Bunratty Castle in County Limerick is the setting for extremely popular banquets put on just as they might have been the Middle Ages. The food is served by young men and women in medieval costume and except for a knife to cut the bread, no other utensils are needed. However, the warm, moist towel provided after the main course most certainly is! It is a memorable evening and, except for the castle setting or the serving vassals in costume, it would be simple to put on a similar spread such as the following. To make it even more authentic, serve the meal with plenty of Bunratty Meade.

Soup: Leek and Potato Soup*
Entrée: Heather and Honey Spareribs,*served with bowls of honey for dipping
Accompaniment: St. Brigid's Oaten Bread*
Dessert: Carolans Irish Blondies.*

Elegant Irish Fare
Appetizer: Angels on Horseback* and Avocado with Guinness Mayonnaise*
Soup: Smoked Salmon Bisque*
Entrée: Guinness Basted Roast Lamb*
Vegetables: Roast potatoes and medley of garden vegetables
Salad: Mushroom Salad with Meade*
Accompaniment: Traditional White Soda Bread*
Dessert: Irish Whiskey Trifle.

Note: For companies, products or services mentioned in this chapter, please consult:

The Resource Listing in Section VI
The North American Celtic Buyers Association website.
If you live in the United States or Canada, they have a great
search function that will enable you to find the nearest Irish shop:
www.celticbuyers.com
My website:
www.irishcultureandcustoms.com/Weddings/WeddingRsrcs.html

5

THE CEREMONY

Wherever you plan to be married and whatever your spiritual leanings, there are ways you can bind and bless your union that will express your devotion as well as reflect your Irish heritage. Granted, there are traditional rituals which must be observed if one is to be married within a certain religious denomination. To avoid any disappointment, consult with your celebrant. Find out very early in the planning stages what will be permitted in the way of music, decor, vows, and so on. In most instances, a wedding is such a joyous occasion, the chances are excellent that you will be given a lot of flexibility.

Basic to all of the elements that go into planning a wedding is the ceremony. But all too often, amidst the frenetic activity that accompanies every other aspect, from selecting a gown to deciding where to have the reception, organizing the most important event of the day doesn't always get the attention it deserves. As a result, many contemporary weddings have a sameness about them.

To avoid a cookie-cutter celebration, focus on what will help make yours as Irish as possible. In ancient Ireland, for example, ceremonies took place outside. So, you might want to consider a garden wedding. Or, reflective of weddings a few hundred years ago, you could have the ceremony in the family home of either the bride or the groom.

These days, most couples choose to be married in a house of worship, but even here, you could draw from twelfth-century Irish history and perhaps, if it's allowed, arrange for the ceremony to be performed right outside the church door. Or, if the budget permits it, and you'd like to follow in the footsteps of many an Irish bride and groom, you could be married at St Patrick's Irish National Church in

Rome. This has several practical advantages including saving the cost of a reception, eliminating emotional stress if your families don't get along, and staying in one of the most romantic cities in Europe to start your honeymoon. If you would like to do this, you must first contact your parish priest because all documents, your baptismal certificates, for example, must be sent to St. Patrick's through a diocesan office. Once you are certain of having all of the necessary paperwork, reward your priest with a generous donation for his efforts on your behalf and then contact St. Patrick's. They will inform you of available dates and will also assist you with securing tickets for a Papal Audience. While tickets are free, they must be booked well in advance.

If you are being married in the Roman Catholic Church, you might wish to have your marriage blessed by the Pope. To receive a Papal Blessing (a certificate signed by an official in Rome on behalf of His Holiness), purchase a blank certificate from a religious book shop, fill in the necessary details and send it to the Vatican at least three

To ensure a fine day for the wedding, there are three slightly different customs involving the Infant of Prague, a religious statue which is often displayed in more traditional Irish Roman Catholic homes.
The first is to place the statue outside under a bush the night before and if the statue is found headless next day, the sun will shine.
(What may help, of course, is that the heads on these statues are notoriously prone to falling off!).
Another version is to put the statue in the hallway of the bride's home with a unit of paper currency underneath it. The third custom is to place the statue to one side of the church door(s) on the wedding morning.

Still another way a Roman Catholic household will endeavour to ensure good weather is to place rosary beads in a window one week before the wedding. Many families will also place a small statue of the Blessed Mother on the window sill. This is done with great piety and prayers are said all week long to Our Lady. Otherwise, according to the Irish woman who contributed this custom, it will rain for sure!

months in advance of your wedding, especially if you want to have it on the exact date.

Wherever your nuptials take place, many key elements associated with today's contemporary ceremonies can be given an Irish feel and flavor. And if your wedding fantasy is to be married in Ireland, check out the section in this chapter on how to make your dream a reality.

CEREMONIAL MASSES

When I was growing up, I automatically assumed that if you were Irish you were also Roman Catholic. I've long since learned that nationality and geography don't always determine religious or spiritual leanings. For those of you, however, who will be having a Roman Catholic ceremony, you might consider the following Masses, or parts of them, while the suggestions regarding vows and blessings can be easily adapted to suit most denominations.

St. Patrick's Mass by composer/conductor Philip Green. Blending Gregorian chants with classical choir music and traditional Irish airs, it's a powerful composition that's best performed if you have access to many musicians, a great choir and a superb Irish tenor. Since that's out of the question for most couples, consider excerpting pieces from:

The Mass of St. Francis of Assisi - Let Me Bring Love. While Mr. Green wrote this Mass for children to perform, an adult choir could easily evoke the same deep emotional quality of the simple melodies. And if you don't have access to a choir, but you can get a really good soloist who can lead the responses, then definitely consider:

The Celtic Mass composed by Christopher Walker. He's a British composer/conductor/lecturer who now lives in the United States. We used this Mass for our daughter's wedding and it was easy to blend in all of the other Irish melodies we had selected. As far as I know, while Mr. Green's Masses have been recorded, The *Celtic Mass* has not. However, the sheet music is available.

Alternatively to any of these compositions, you may wish to consider having your Mass celebrated the old-fashioned way, in Latin! Be sure to check with your celebrant to see if this would be permitted. If so, it should definitely please elderly family members who may, as with many in their age group, be sentimentally attached to how the Mass was celebrated in Ireland and elsewhere just a few decades ago.

PRAYERS

Traditional prayer said when going to Mass

Hail to thee, O Church of God, in which lives my Saviour, Jesus Christ. May Mary and the twelve apostles pray for me today.

From St. Patrick's Breastplate

Christ be with me, Christ within me
Christ behind me, Christ before me
Christ beside me, Christ to win me
Christ to comfort and restore me
Christ beneath me, Christ above me
Christ in quiet, Christ in danger
Christ in hearts of all that love me
Christ in mouth of friend and stranger.

Prayer for protection

Be the eye of God dwelling with you
The foot of Christ in guidance with you
The shower of the Spirit pouring on you
Richly and generously.

Traditional prayer when departing the church after Mass

Farewell O Mary, and farewell, O Christ!
May Ye preserve my soul until I come again.

In the old days, young men carried torches of bogwood to light the bride on her journey to her new home. Based on tradition, some Irish brides today are led up the aisle by their attendants carrying large, lighted candles. These are then placed around the altar to illuminate the bride and groom throughout the ceremony.

BLESSINGS

A morning blessing adapted for a wedding ceremony

We believe, O God of all Gods,
That thou art the eternal Father of life.
We believe, O God of all good,
That Thou art the eternal Father of Love.
We believe, O Lord and God of the peoples,
That thou art the creator of the high heavens,
That Thou are the creator of the skies above,
That Thou art creator of the oceans below.
We believe, O Lord and God of the peoples,
That Thou art He who created our souls
and set their warp,
Who created our bodies from dust and from ashes,
Who gave to our bodies our breath and to our
souls their possession.
Father, bless to us our bodies.
Father, bless to us our souls.
Father, bless to us our lives.
Father, bless to us our beliefs.

From the religious songs of Connacht

The blessing of Mary and the blessing of God,
the blessing of the sun and the moon on their road,
of the man in the east and the man in the west
and my blessing with thee and be thou blest.

Blessing for love and protection

May the love and protection
Jesus, His mother and St. Patrick can give
Be yours in abundance
As long as you live.

In an Irish Catholic Nuptial Mass, it has become the custom
for the bride and groom to exchange silver and gold coins.
It would seem appropriate to do this just before the exchange
of rings. They each say to each other: "I give you this gold
and silver, symbols of all I possess."

CONTRIBUTED BY KEVIN & YVONNE HANRAHAN

Blessing from a statue of St. Patrick in County Mayo
May St. Patrick smile upon you,
The Lord above bless you,
And peace and contentment
Forever possess you.

Blessing for the bride and groom
Length of life and sunny days
And may your souls not go homewards
until your own child falls in love.

Blessing for a bride to her groom and vice versa
You are the star of each night,
You are the brightness of every morning,
You are the story of each guest,
You are the report of every land.
No evil shall befall you, on hill nor bank,
In field or valley, on mountain or in glen.
Neither above, nor below, neither in sea,
Nor on shore,
In skies above, nor in the depths.
You are the kernel of my heart,
You are the face of my sun,
You are the harp of my music,
You are the crown of my company.

Traditional Irish marriage blessing

May God go with you and bless you,
May you see your children's children,
May you be poor in misfortune and rich in blessings,
May you know nothing but happiness from this
day forward.

Variation on the traditional marriage blessing

May you be poor in misfortune,
Rich in blessings,
Slow to make enemies,
Quick to make friends.
But rich or poor, quick or slow,
May you know nothing but happiness from this day forward,
And may you live to be a hundred years
with one extra year to repent.

READINGS

If yours is to be a Roman Catholic ceremony which includes the celebration of the Mass, you will be required to have a reading from the Old Testament and one from the New Testament. Other denominations may also require readings from the scriptures - check with your celebrant. If you do have the flexibility to select non-biblical readings, or a mixture of both, consider including one or more of the Irish prayers and blessings above. Do you know a friend or relative who can read and speak Irish? Why not ask them to do a reading while another friend or relative translates it into English, line by line. Accompanied by soft harp music, this could be both spiritually uplifting and emotionally stirring.

VOWS

While most couples choose traditional wedding vows, if it's permitted by your celebrant, why not draw from old literature and poetry and write your own or adapt from the following fine examples, the first three of which are from old Irish folklore:

By the power that Christ brought from heaven,
mayst thou love me.
As the sun follows its course, mayst thou follow me.
As light to the eye, as bread to the hungry, as joy to the heart,
may thy presence be with me, O one that I love,
till death comes to part us asunder.

O Christ, by your five wounds, by the nine orders of angels, if this woman is ordained for me, let me hold her hand now, and breathe her breath. O my love. I pray to the top of your head, to the sole of your foot, to each side of your breast, that you may not leave me or forsake me. As a foal after the mare, as a child after the mother, may you follow, and stay with me till death comes to part us asunder. Amen.

O woman (man) loved by me, mayst thou give me thy heart, thy soul and thy body. Amen.

From an old Irish poem

My love is no short year's sentence.
It is grief lodged under the skin,
Strength pushed beyond its bounds;
The four quarters of the world,
The highest point of heaven.
It is
A heart breaking or
Battle with a ghost,
Outrunning the sky or
Courting an echo.
So is my love, my passion
& my devotion
To him (her) to whom I give them.

Druidic vow for unity

We swear by peace and love to stand
Heart to heart and hand in hand.
Mark, O Spirit, and hear us now,
Confirming this our sacred vow.

Promise between a bride and groom

Bride: To wed me, your promise I must be certain of, so that we
may live out our lives in sweet contentment, love.

Groom: Here is my hand to hold with you, to bind us for life so
that I'll grow old with you.

Another lovely vow possibility

Don't walk in front of me, I may not follow,
Don't walk behind me, I may not lead,
Walk beside me and be my friend.

This is attributed to Albert Camus who was born in Algeria. It's
included here because of its tremendous popularity in Ireland and
elsewhere. In fact, our daughter used this same quotation on the back
of her program.

DECOR

For altar and church decor, be sure to consult with your
celebrant as to whether or not any of the following suggestions will be
permitted.

Banners/Flags

Display the Irish flag on one side of the altar and the national flag
of your country on the other. Or, you could have a talented
seamstress create banners decorated with Celtic emblems, your names,
and the wedding date. Hanging vertical banners on either side of an
altar can be very effective, especially if they are color-coordinated with
your flowers and bridal party attire. After the ceremony, banners can
play double duty as part of the decor for your reception. Later, they will
become wonderful family heirlooms to bring out on special occasions,
such as the christening of your first child.

Bells

If you are to be married in a church and it is permitted by the denomination, the chime of wedding bells as the bridal party leaves is an old tradition in many parts of the world. It was thought that the sound of bells had the power to ward off evil spirits, so it's worth checking into! Alternatively, if your ceremony venue makes it impossible to have the peal of bells accompany your recessional, you might consider giving each guest a tiny bell which they can ring as the bridal party exits. This might also be a better choice than throwing confetti, birdseed or flower petals, which, in many places, isn't allowed anymore. In addition to warding off evil spirits, there's another old Irish superstition that the sound of a bell will 'break the silence' and eliminate any discord between a couple. As a result, a bell has become a traditional Irish wedding gift.

Flowers

If, as with most engaged couples, you are to be married in a church or chapel and will call on the services of a professional florist, he or she will most likely recommend coordinating your altar arrangements with all of your other flowers, from bouquets to baskets. However, for a charming extra touch, consider placing a wreath or pair of wreaths made from dried Irish flowers on the front door(s). Or, if yours is to be a Roman Catholic ceremony, incorporate the Irish tradition of honoring the Virgin Mother by placing a wreath at the foot of her statue.

If you've decided on an outdoor wedding, in a garden perhaps, or by the ocean, don't be shy about recognizing your proud heritage. If your family of old was tied to the land, consider honoring that with sheafs of wheat. In the old days, following a wedding, friends of the bride and groom would often decorate the bridal bed in flowers of the season and stalks of straw which were harbingers of plenty. If your ancestors were fishermen, you could ask your florist to incorporate appropriate marine elements. For example, were your ancestors Galway seafarers? The red sails of their 'hooker' fishing vessels could become the foundation from which to create a dramatically different look for an outdoor ceremony. I hope that these suggestions will encourage you to search out your own roots and perhaps help you find unique ways to honor your ancestors' memory.

To show love and respect for a relative who is recently deceased, Kim McGuire offers this poignant suggestion in her planner, *The Irish Wedding Book:* If possible, visit the cemetery before you head out for the reception and place a special bouquet at your loved one's final resting place.

Pew Bows

It has become customary at many Irish weddings to attach a bow at the end of every pew, or at the end of the pews where the families will be seated. Often the bows are accented with flowers or trailing tendrils of ivy. If this is an extra touch you wish to add to your decor, let your florist know. It will increase the cost, but in general, most florists will include pew bows as part of the floral package.

PROGRAMS

As with all of your other wedding stationery, from invitations to place cards, your program design should make a very personal, as well as Irish statement. Too often, though, the program is put together in a hurry and often ends up being nothing more than a single sheet of photocopied paper. With a little planning, however, you can have a lovely program that guests will want to keep as a memento. Many of the invitation companies sell programs that will compliment your invitations, but if you're on a strict budget, it may be less expensive to design and make your own. It will also be easier to incorporate Irish elements that may not be available otherwise. See Information Section IV for a program that's easy to make.

RING CUSHION

Several catalogs offer Irish-inspired ring cushions, including at least two which feature the Claddagh symbol. Alternatively, if the Claddagh design is not part of your plans, may I suggest a plain white or off-white cushion which you can customize exactly to your liking with Irish linen and lace derived from a ready-made doily or handkerchief.

UNITY CANDLE/MOTHERS' CANDLES

Lighting a Unity Candle is a relatively modern custom which has become very popular. Many couples are choosing a three-candle arrangement and, when the time comes to light the large center candle, the bride and groom use the lit candles on either side to light the one in the center. They can then either blow out the two small candles or leave them burning for the duration of the ceremony. As of this writing, there are many resources on the internet where you can purchase candles with a an Irish or Celtic design.

While this is not an Irish tradition, it is becoming more and more common for the mothers to light the candles on either side of the Unity candle. The most appropriate time to do this is before the ceremony begins.

Note: If possible, see if you can find candles made of beeswax. Beekeeping was once very common in rural Ireland and there's an old superstition that if you neglect to tell the bees important news (such as an upcoming wedding), the bees will swarm and fly away. I doubt if telling a pair of candles will have the same impact, but for good luck, tell your mothers to whisper the good news as they light the candles.

MUSIC

If it's within your budget, hire musicians who specialize in traditional Irish music. Or, if the location where your wedding will be held has a decent sound system, you could use pre-recorded tapes or CDs. Whether you decide on live musicians or pre-recorded selections, there's so much wonderful Irish music available that your challenge will be in choosing which pieces to play. Whatever you select, do resist the urge to use *She Moved Through the Fair*. It's a well-known traditional air with words by Padraic Colum, but while it's beautiful, the young girl who so poignantly reminds the young man that "It will not be long, love, before our wedding day" is a ghost! In Information Section I (music) is a listing of suggestions appropriate to key parts of a traditional ceremony, from the prelude to the recessional, as well as the words to *The Irish Wedding Song*. Written by an Australian, Ian Betteridge (who also composed the music), the piece was initially played on Irish radio programs and it has since become very popular at Irish weddings all over the world. Many brides of Irish descent are incorporating it into their ceremony, and they often include the words in their program so that family and friends can sing it together. If you are not permitted to include secular music during the ceremony, you might want to consider having the guests sing this at an appropriate moment during your reception.

Irish Dancers

For a touch of pageantry and drama, consider hiring a group of Irish dancers in full regalia to greet guests as they arrive at the church. They could hand out programs, take charge of the guest book and later, they could dance at your reception.

Piper

To set the stage for the lovely Irish music to come (and if your budget allows it), hire a piper to play as your guests arrive. But be sure to hire a musician who plays the uilleann pipes which are very different from Scottish bagpipes. After the ceremony, as the bridal party exits, have your piper pick up the recessional melody until the bridal party and guests have left the church. If your receiving line will be at the church, the piper can continue playing. Afterwards, perhaps while you are having photos taken, the piper could go on to your reception venue and be there to greet guests as they arrive.

If the reception is being held within walking distance of the church, arrange for the piper to lead the way. You might also want to consider having members of the wedding party follow the piper, carrying banners or flags. For a real Irish touch, consider riding to your reception in a horse-drawn carriage with your guests following you on foot or in cars. Do you live in the country and does the groom know how to ride a horse? For a truly old-fashioned Irish departure, lead the procession behind the piper and head for your reception on horseback!

In general, regarding your choice of music, if your place of worship has a music director, organist or choir leader, do take advantage of their knowledge. Tell them you are planning an Irish celebration and you may discover, as I did, that they can share a wealth of suggestions and recommendations.

Except for those specific details demanded by your own spiritual community, your ceremony can be completely Irish, from beginning to end. Work closely with your celebrant and together you will create a service that you, your families, and your friends will long remember.

*Under ancient Irish law, women were allowed to retain
their maiden name after marriage, if they so desired.
Today, many professional women follow this old practice
without realizing that it's steeped in Irish tradition.*

*After the exchange of wedding bands, there is a contemporary custom
where the bride and groom exchange coins as a symbol of their
worldly goods. If the coins clink as they are exchanged,
the couple will have many children.*

*A man should never sing at his own wedding.
Neither should his bride.
It's unlucky.*

A VOW RENEWAL WITH THE SOUND AND FEEL OF IRELAND

When my husband and I were married decades ago, it didn't occur to either one of us to have an Irish wedding. His family had been in the United States for centuries and, even though their last name is Haggerty. they consider themselves to be 'Swamp Yankees.'

My parents, while first-generation Irish, were living in England and my dad was too ill to travel. Understandably, my mother was too worried about him to give much thought to a wedding. Without the influence of a mother-of-the-bride, my plans were very much boiler plate 'Here Comes The Bride.' But, for our next milestone anniversary, it will be different. We will renew our vows and the celebration will be as Irish as we can make it.

The idea came about after I made the acquaintance of Linda Schmidt. She had bought the first edition of *The Traditional Irish Wedding* because she was looking for ideas to incorporate into her own vow-renewal celebration. In fact, Linda is very creative and came up with so many great ideas, I asked her if she would allow me to include the details in the next edition of my book. She graciously consented. Herewith, Linda's dream-come-true Irish wedding - a dozen years later.

It all started when we wanted to do a renewal of vows for our 10th anniversary but plans just never finalized. When our 12th anniversary came around, we decided then would be a good opportunity to do what we had wanted to do before - an Irish ceremony with the sound and feel of Ireland. We were in a better financial situation as well and that meant that we could do what we wanted without worrying about money. What follows is a synopsis of how it all came together.

LINDA'S DREAM COME TRUE

Flowers

I wanted something very simple. I didn't want a typical bouquet that was round. I wanted something that looked like I went out into the fields of Ireland, picked my own flowers, and created a small bouquet of my own. While the bouquet turned out to be somewhat larger than I expected, it was still beautiful and easy to carry. I selected flowers that would be Irish: Bells of Ireland and Heather. I also chose Summer Flower (a small white bloom with a yellow middle on long stems), Misty (a purple flower that grows almost looking like a pretty weed) and Plumosa (a feathery looking greenery). My husband's daughter, Autumn, was also in the ceremony to carry the box with the rings in it. I had a headpiece made for her that included the same blossoms that were in my bouquet. I then ordered six baskets of heather to decorate the church. The baskets I chose were rustic looking and the florist made them look as if they were over-flowing with blossoms. I had wanted live heather plants but was advised that they don't grow very full or flowery. The baskets worked out perfectly.

Wedding Rings

We have always wanted matching bands but we just couldn't afford them for our wedding. But, now we could. I found the most beautiful pair of rings I've ever seen in the Gaelsong catalogue. They are white gold trimmed in yellow gold and have matching designs from Ireland. They are called Tara Wedding Bands. After they arrived a month before they were expected (a good omen), we had them engraved. My husband and I have a phrase we always say to each other, and we wanted that phrase translated into Irish and engraved inside our rings. I found that the phrase "Love you bunches" is not easily translated! So, with the help of my good friend, Bridget and an Irish language instructor from Ireland, Liam, we came up with *"Is tú mo ghrá"* - You are my love. I loved the rings and the engraving so much, and what they stood for, I was as excited about our vow renewal ceremony as I was on our wedding day. I couldn't wait to wear my new ring and show off my "new married life."

Invitation

The invitation we designed was a lesson in patience for myself. I left the details to be decided by my husband and he did a good job. It was the calligrapher we hired who had no imagination. We gave her the words we wanted to say and for $40 an hour, she penned a beautifully lettered copy of them. However, they were in the exact order and line for line that we gave her. We paid her for her time and soon discovered a very expensive lesson. Don't just give the words to the person, but lay it out as well. I expected her to come up with a good-looking design layout with some attractive alternatives, but she did not. What we ended up doing was our own design with a newly purchased Kells Font Set for Windows and a little imagination. I have to say that we were very pleased at the results and received several compliments. We were also going to have a dinner at a restaurant afterwards and needed to include directions on how to get there. I found the most wonderful break-apart cards at the copiers that were not too heavy to put through my printer. Everyone was amazed that we did them ourselves. They thought a professional had done them. I found some wonderful Celtic knot envelope seal stickers from an Irish gift store that I used to seal the back of the envelopes, and on the front I used heart-shaped postage stamps.

Invitation wording

As the endless knot has no beginning and no end,
so our love cannot be divided
nor broken with age.

Just as the precious metal
from which the wedding band is forged
cannot be dimmed
nor its color altered by the passage of time,
so the bonds of love
cannot be loosened or diminished.

Roy and Linda Schmidt wish to invite you
to witness the renewal of their vows
of love and loyalty affirmed so long ago.

Aisle Runner

I purchased a Celtic knot stencil that I wanted to use on the aisle runner edges. I quickly learned why I had never seen anything like this in any of my catalogs. I'm not sure it can be done. Afterwards, I had to laugh at everything I had tried and purchased, only to find that it wouldn't work. If you know an easy way to stencil, this would have made a wonderful addition to the aisle runner. I tried using a brush, but the paint ran underneath the stencil. I tried spray paint, but as it dried, the paint just ran together even with the lightest of spray. Then I thought I had found the answer. A small foam roller worked wonderfully in my test runs, but after an hour of being very careful, one of the designs ran under the stencil and I couldn't fix it. The runner was ruined. The runner I used was textured slightly and could have been the reason the paint ran under the stencil. I see a terrific business opportunity here if someone can make it work.

Music

I have a rather extensive collection of Celtic CDs and it was so much fun going through them all to pick just the right songs. Some of the music I selected to play while people were being seated is not exactly Irish, but has a Celtic feel to it. I made a tape of the music and it was played continuously. We had originally wanted to have an outdoor ceremony at the church using their patio area which has a beautiful view of the mountains, a built-in creek with waterfall and plants and flowers. However, when we tested the music outside, the sound was lost. When we played the music using a good quality boombox inside the church, the sound was awesome. I've included at the end a listing of the music we used.

Ceremony

We would be taking wine during the ceremony, and for that we used a pewter goblet featuring an endless knot design. Our choice of libation was Bunratty Meade. We also lined the box carrying the rings with an embroidered linen hanky from Ireland.

It was a very simple ceremony which began with an invocation, the statement of intentions, and this blessing:

May you be blessed with the strength of heaven
The light of the sun and the radiance of the moon
The splendor of fire, the speed of lightning
The swiftness of wind, the depth of the sea
The stability of the earth and the firmness of rock.

For the actual vow renewal, our pastor first asked my husband Roy:
"Roy, will you reaffirm your vow to Linda to be your wife, to live
together according to God's plan? Do you promise to love and
honor her, respect and defend her, strengthen and forgive her,
and give yourself only to her so long as you both shall live?"

Roy answers:
"This I pledge to do with the help of God. From this life to the
next - *Ó n saol seo go dtí an saol eile*. (Pronunciation: ohn
see-ul shuh guh djee on see-il ell-eh)

Roy sips from the goblet.

The pastor then repeated the same question to me. I give the same
response as Roy's and I also sip from the goblet.

For our vow and exchange of rings, Roy said:
"I, Roy, in the presence of God and these witnesses take you,
Linda, to be my wife. I pledge you my love and faithfulness
according to God's plan until we are parted by death. Two
wedding rings together form the simplest and strongest of the
endless knots. My love for you thus enshrined shall be
everlasting; from this day forward into the life beyond."
Then it was my turn:
"I, Linda, in the presence of God and these witnesses take you,
Roy, to be my husband. I pledge you my love and faithfulness
according to God's plan until we are parted by death. All things
in life have a beginning. In Irish tradition, the endless knot
stands for prosperity and long life. It has no end. This ring I
present to you has no end and is a symbol of my love for you
and the life we will continue to have together."

Reception

After the wonder and splendor of the ceremony was over, the last thing was the reception. We considered using a caterer that was recommended to us by the florist, but we found that while the cost would be almost the same as taking everyone out to a restaurant, we had to consider the time of year. If it rained, which was looking very likely, we would have to entertain a crowd of people in our house, which isn't that big. Also, the time of day had to be considered. It was going to be 5pm and getting dark and we didn't have adequate lighting, so the restaurant won our decision. The caterer would have been nice to have because I was looking at some of the wonderful recipes in *The Traditional Irish Wedding* and had selected several dishes that the caterer could have made. She was also willing to throw in some Irish decorations, too, since it was only a month before St. Patrick's Day. But we decided to contact some restaurants and the best price we got was only $1 per person more than the caterer would have been by the time we figured in all the tables, chairs, awning, lights, etc. The restaurant offered our guests a menu with their choice of chicken, salmon or steak with a caesar salad, bread and beverage. Everyone had a good time.

And now for the final thing-to-go-wrong-but-it-wouldn't-be-a-proper-wedding-if-something-didn't-go-wrong problem. We were delighted that everyone we asked had accepted. We invited a total of 29 people and with children, it came to 36 people. Still not a problem. When we called in the reservation confirmation total to the restaurant, my husband told them 38 just in case we had someone bring their kids and forget to tell us. Not a problem. The problem came when my husband, his daughter, my mother-in-law and myself showed up at the restaurant; there were, as expected 35 people there since the 36th person invited was my mother-in-law and she was with us. She sat in one empty seat which left 2 empty seats. Well, there was one of us who didn't have a chair. When we called the restaurant, we neglected to add in ourselves to the number of people that would be there. We had given them the number of those we invited! It was really funny when we discovered what we had done and had to rearrange the tables.

However, the funniest thing that happened was at the end of the evening when we were leaving the restaurant, which by now was full of people. One lady came up to me and complimented me on my outfit. I wore a dress called Amethyst and Velvet and a dark red velvet cape. I had a padded halo with dried flowers on it and long ribbons down the back that I had made for another event. I thanked her and told her we had just renewed our vows. She said, "Really? I thought you were in a play." We wanted to have an Irish theme and the garments we wore reflected that. The outfit my husband wore was a billowy muslin shirt with a leather thong tie, a green vest tied with a leather thong, black fencing pants and knee-hi leather Renaissance boots. His daughter wore a green peasant dress that has a girdle tied in front and long bell sleeves. You'll find many outfits similar to these in the Museum Replicas Limited catalogue.

Overall, the entire celebration was a big success, and I finally got my wish for an Irish-themed event. It was well worth the wait!

CONTRIBUTED BY LINDA SCHMIDT

Playlist

While people were being seated:

Ring of Magic Fairy from *Fairy of the Woods* by Gary Stadler

Forest Dark'n from *Fairy of the Woods* by Gary Stadler

Goodbye Mrs. Goodavich/Rosie's Reel from *Otherworld* by Lunasa

Tea House Moon from *The Memory of Trees* by Enya

Watermark from *Watermark* by Enya

Celtic Vision - entire CD

Processional:

Nightsong from *Fairy Nightsongs* by Gary Stadler

Recessional:

The Cat's Meow from *Songs of the Irish Whistle 2* by Joannie Madden

GETTING MARRIED IN IRELAND

Have you ever considered having your dream wedding in Ireland? You are not alone. The days of quickie Vegas weddings, cookie-cutter ceremonies and corporate hotel receptions are on the way out. Modern couples want a unique wedding location and vacation they can enjoy together with their intimate circle of family and close friends.

While the average American wedding can easily cost US$20,000 for just one evening, couples are finding they can spend four days celebrating with their guests in Ireland for half of that cost.

It is no surprise that so many couples and international celebrities are opting to escape to Ireland for their dream weddings. The short, five hour flight from the US makes it both accessible and irresistible. And a destination wedding takes the pressure off the couple and their families because no one is hosting from their home or hometown, so local distractions are immediately eliminated. The scene is set for a dream vacation for everyone in attendance.

If you intend to have a wedding with more than ten guests traveling to Ireland, I would strongly suggest you get some professional assistance. Assistance may include a specialized travel agent or an Irish wedding coordinator. Although it can be hard work if you pursue planning without professional help, it can be done. Some coordinators like myself offer a vendor and locations list for a minimal fee. This is a great option for couples with experience in planning or who may be working with a tight budget because you have access to the top Irish vendors and you get the pre-negotiated rates.

However, most couples have little or no experience in planning an event or wedding. Finding the perfect location, hiring the top local vendors and organizing a wedding in another country may seem daunting. But with the skills and experience of a good coordinator, planning your wedding in Ireland will be easy and even fun. When shopping for a coordinator, look for a company that works on a flat fee system to protect yourself from inflated 'estimate work' (hourly rates and percentages). Be sure to get a written contract that states exactly what you will be paying. You don't want to be surprised by the bill on your special day. There are very strict legal guidelines for getting married in Ireland and an experienced coordinator is essential for guidance and also for helping to simplify this process. Hiring a wedding coordinator could be one of the best decisions you make for peace of mind as well as making your budget go further.

Procedures for a Legal Marriage in Ireland

All couples intending to marry legally in the Republic of Ireland must make written notification in person or by mail to the local Registrar 90 days before the marriage is to take place. If you have access to the internet, you may download this notification form at: www.groireland.ie

After you've secured an officiate and/or location for your ceremony in Ireland, you should request the contact information for the local Registrar. Once this notification is received by the Registrar, you will be sent a receipt which you will need to bring to Ireland for the ceremony. The ceremony may be either religious or civil.

Religious Ceremony

This ceremony is performed by a religious officiate inside a church or building that is licensed, certified or registered for marriages. It is governed by the religious rules and requirements of the particular church you choose. Often a couple is required to provide religious certification from their affiliate church.

There is no residency requirement for a religious ceremony; however, most churches have weddings planned up to a year in advance and all of them require that you speak directly to the local officiate regarding your plans before you make your official written notification to the Registrar 90 days before the wedding may take place.

Civil Ceremony

This ceremony is performed by the local Registrar inside the Registrar's office or an agreed upon location in the area. This is a new law that is due to go into effect late August 2004. This would be the same Registrar to whom you will make your 90- day written notification.

For a civil ceremony you must also fulfill a residency requirement before you can make your written notification. There are two ways to meet this residency requirement:

1. By License: This requires that the couple meet with the Registrar in person and then stay in the district area together for 15 days before a marriage ceremony may take place.

2. By Certificate: This requires that the couple meet with the Registrar in person and then stay in the district area together for seven days. Twenty one days after this residency requirement is met, the couple may return to the district for the marriage ceremony (Two visits to Ireland).

All legal marriages in Ireland are recognized in the United States. If you live in a different location, be sure to check the applicable laws in your country.

Blessing Ceremony

Many couples are opting to marry legally in their own country, considering this portion as paperwork, and having a formal, non-legal ceremony in Ireland at the location of their choice. This works well because you do not have to meet residency, legal or religious requirements.

Locations

Ireland lends itself to many unique ceremony styles and wedding locations. I've arranged everything from a medieval-themed wedding in a castle with the bride and groom sporting matching swords, to an ancient Celtic hand-fasting on the Cliffs of Moher, officiated by a monk from the Aran Islands. Most of my clients are American and they are choosing locations that are within easy driving distance of either Shannon or Dublin airport. This is because they have little or no experience driving on the left side of the road and they want to keep driving time to a minimum. The west of Ireland, including Counties Limerick, Clare, and Galway, is full of charming seaside villages that are off the beaten path. Counties Dublin, Wicklow, Meath, and Kildare offer magnificent castle residences within driving distance of bustling Dublin City.

Whether you're married in luxury in the formal gardens of one of Ireland's five-star castle hotels, or celebrating an intimate ceremony inside a charming chapel, the Irish will embrace your desire to experience their rich and vibrant culture. The Irish have a fierce pride in their heritage and there is an abundance of information on tradition, art, poetry, music and language that can play an essential role in your Irish wedding.

Good Luck in your planning!

CONTRIBUTED BY ANNE LANIER
OF ANNE LANIER WEDDINGS

LEAVING THE CHURCH

An old custom was for the bridegroom to toss a handful of coins to children who would gather and wait for the couple to come out.

It was once traditional in County Galway for all the neighbors to light small bonfires along the side of the road which the bridal party will see as the cars go by. This custom is meant as a wish that the newlyweds will have good luck, warmth and many children.

It used to be the custom to shower the newlyweds with flower petals for good luck.

After the ceremony, it was once common in parts of Ireland for young girls to present the bride with horseshoes made of stiff silver paper looped with long white ribbons. But they had to be sure the horseshoes were presented turned up as this would hold in the luck.

Note: For companies, products or services mentioned in this chapter, please consult:

The Resource Listing in Section VI
The North American Celtic Buyers Association website.
If you live in the United States or Canada, they have a great
search function that will enable you to find the nearest Irish shop:
www.celticbuyers.com
My website:
www.irishcultureandcustoms.com/Weddings/WeddingRsrcs.html

6

THE NEWEST OF FOOD
AND THE OLDEST OF DRINK
RECEPTION

"In Haley's house the wedding was, and people who were there told me it was a fine turn-out. No expense spared, this and that there, currany toops and whatnots, all kinds of grudles, buns, trifle and that shaky shivery stuff you ate with a spoon..."

In the old days, receptions were held at home and customarily, just as it is today, it was the bride's parents who hosted the festivities. After the ceremony, the couple would either walk from the church to the house or, if they could afford it, they'd ride in a carriage. All of the guests would follow behind - on foot, in carriages, or on horseback - a procession that was customarily called 'wedding drag.'

If you can accommodate the guest list, or if there are areas outside where tents can be set up, a reception at the house would be in keeping with tradition. But, regardless of where you have your reception, and no matter how elaborate or simple, good luck will surely follow if the hospitality of the house is extended to all. It's not practical nowadays, but long ago, everyone in an Irish village was invited to the festivities which lasted all day, well into the night, and often didn't end until the next morning. It was a great boast in the old days to have it said that 'we danced til daylight.'

Apparently, this custom is still going strong in certain parts of Ireland. A word of caution, though, about excessive drinking. It was considered a great insult to the family of the house and the bridal couple if a wedding guest overindulged. In fact, a friend of the family was always given the dual responsibility of seeing to it that everyone had something to drink while at the same time watching for any signs of 'weakness,' a euphemism my father used to describe someone who was making a little too merry with the libations.

Within this section, you'll find suggestions for decor, music, toasts and the wedding feast, alphabetized where appropriate. In Information Section III, there's a calendar of special days in the Irish year and the foods traditionally served, and the Resource Listing in Section VI will tell you where to purchase favors, music, and all of the ingredients - food and otherwise - for 'a fine turn out.'

BLESSINGS

If appropriate, ask your celebrant to say Grace or give a blessing before the feast begins, and perhaps afterwards. In keeping with tradition, the following old Irish blessings could serve you well.

A bride is known to have power over 'the good people' unless she takes both feet off the ground during the festivities. If she does, the 'good people' will regain the upper hand.

At the reception, it was customary for the groom to be carried around in a 'jaunting car' (chair) and presented to the guests as a married man. The groom would be seated in the chair and then two of the strongest groomsmen would lift the chair up as high as they could manage and parade the groom around.

It is traditional to give a newlywed couple a crystal wedding bowl symbolizing wealth, health and happiness. Legend has it that as long as the bowl is safe and secure, the family will be blessed with the laughter of a child, the health of a lion, and coins in their purses.

Blessings before the meal

May the blessing of the five loaves and two fishes, which God divided amongst five thousand men, be ours; and may the King who made the division put luck back in our food and in our portion. Amen.

The grace of God and the favor of St. Patrick on all that we see and all that we do. The blessing that God put on the five loaves and two fishes, may He put on this food.

Bless us, O Lord, bless our food and drink,
You who has so dearly redeemed us
And has saved us from evil,
As you have given us this share of food,
May you give us our share of everlasting glory.

Blessing after the meal
Praise to the King of Plenty,
Praise every time to God,
A hundred praises and thanks to Jesus Christ,
For what we have eaten and shall eat.

A blessing on everyone
As plentiful as the grass that grows
Or the sand on the shore,
Or the dew on the lea,
So the blessings of the King of Grace
On every soul that was, that is, or will be.

Blessing at the end of the reception
That the roll call this day twelve months may find us all present and none absent.

DECOR AND ACCESSORIES

Whether your reception is held at home, in a large banquet hall, or anywhere else in-between, the Irish theme can easily be adapted to just about any setting. The most important criteria are that your guests will be comfortable, have plenty to eat and drink, that your colors coordinate, and that any Irish symbols you choose to incorporate are handled with good taste.

In the old days, if the wedding was a large one, it was often held in the barn. Tables would be pushed together and arranged so that they ran the length of the building. If you live in a metropolitan city in the United States, there are state and city parks that have lodges which are available for receptions. Many of these are very rustic which makes them ideal for a truly old-fashioned, Irish country wedding. They're also much less expensive than hotels and country clubs and worth looking into if you have similar facilities in your area.

Banners and the Irish Flag

If, for whatever reason, you couldn't display the Irish flag and/or banners at your ceremony, the reception is most certainly the time to bring them out. I have heard of couples who received a specially made banner with embroidered Celtic designs as a wedding gift. A lovely idea.

Cake Knife and Server

As of this writing, Claddagh design serving utensils are readily available from several sources. Depending on your wedding decor, other designs might be more appropriate; check Irish gift shops, wedding catalogs and the internet for a wide array of styles and patterns.

Cake Topper

Claddaghs, Celtics, musicals, and more are widely available. From porcelain to pewter, it's easy to find the perfect Irish topper for your cake.

Champagne Flutes

Special toasting goblets for the bride and groom are often given as a wedding gift. When they also feature the Claddagh design, they become even more meaningful. There are also many other designs available with an Irish or Celtic theme.

Flowers & Centerpieces

The bridal table should require nothing more than the bouquets of the bridal party set in front of each place setting, facing out so they can be viewed by all of the guests. Special clamps to secure

The custom of strawboys or 'soppers' surprising guests at an Irish celebration is said to date back to the eighteenth century. Masked rustlers preying on the landlord's cattle would escape capture by ducking into a packed wedding reception. In more recent times, strawboys were usually comprised of the menfolk in the wedding party; at some point during the reception they would sneak off, put on long white robes and straw hats which covered their faces. They then returned to the reception and entertained the guests with dancing and other high jinks. In the old days, if you weren't invited to a wedding, you could see the inside of a house for a while by 'strawing it.' Eventually it was considered very lucky if the strawboys showed up.

bouquets to the table can be purchased from most wedding invitation catalogs. While many couples leave the altar arrangements as a gift to the church, in many cases they can't because there's to be another ceremony following theirs. In that event, it would make sense to have the arrangements brought to the reception and, if appropriate, placed on pedestals at either end of the bridal table.

As for the rest of the tables, including the cake table, the simplest approach is to pick up the colors of the bridesmaids' bouquets and follow through. However, depending on the time of year and availability, baskets of shamrocks in full bloom could provide a wonderfully sentimental touch. You could in fact use shamrock that you have grown yourself from seeds that are available in packages from many Irish gift shops.

If yours is to be an evening reception, candlelight is almost essential and hurricane lamps are an elegant, yet inexpensive way to achieve an aura of romance. A talented florist can decorate the lamp bases with wreaths featuring ribbons, flowers and greenery that coordinate with, or match, the wedding party bouquets. If your wedding is taking place in the fall, you might also consider elevating the cabbage to the status of a decorative element by having your florist incorporate the ornamental variety into centerpieces or other floral arrangements.

Irish Flourishes

Instead of the usual name and date inscription (or in addition to), consider using a brief Irish quotation, saying, proverb or line of poetry on paper goods such as cake boxes, napkins, bookmatches and even, perhaps on heavy card stock which is folded in half to create an elegant table tent. See examples of quotations and proverbs throughout this book or in Information Section V. As with the banner idea already mentioned, your initials in a Celtic typeface would also be appropriate.

Setting the Tables

Most reception venues provide tablecloths, napkins and place settings. Generally, linens and china are neutral, which makes it very simple to introduce your own decorative touches. If these items are not provided, the easiest approach is to rent everything from a party rental source or purchase disposable tableware from a wedding invitation catalog. It's truly amazing to see the scope of decorative accessories that are available. From tissue bells to streamers, cake boxes to candy containers, all you need is a little imagination to turn the reception setting into something uniquely yours, and Irish as well!

One old custom in particular can be adapted to your tables and that is to serve a part of the feast in a basket or kish. In many Irish homes, particularly in the north and west, the kish was placed on top of a three-legged pot of hot water to keep food from cooling down too quickly. One couple we know placed a basket of Irish soda

---

Bacachs is another word for strawboys and according to tradition,
only the leader of the group was permitted to speak.
The rest would silently toast the bride and groom
as the leader said in Irish:
'May your family have a family,
And their family have a family,
And may the person who says that your family will not have a family,
never have a family of their own.'

bread on each of the guest tables at their reception. In the old days, you would be certain to offer a loaf that had not been cut into so that your guests would know it was the freshest you had. However, to save time, and make it easier on your guests, it would be best to present it already sliced. Planning a very informal reception? The following idea from an Irish acquaintance could make for a fun and festive atmosphere. At a recent Céilí (Irish dance), she pierced a large baking potato with two miniature Irish flags and placed one on each table.

Planning a large reception? It will be easier for guests to find their seats if you post the seating plan on an easel at the entrance to the room. Alternatively, you can number each table and write out the guests' names and the table number they are assigned to on small cards. Place these in alphabetical order on a table at the entrance and put someone in charge of helping people find their place cards. Your guests, especially the elderly ones, will really appreciate your thoughtfulness. How superstitious are you? When we were writing out the number cards for each table, we purposely omitted thirteen!

As for the head-table seating arrangements at an Irish wedding reception, if you'd like to follow standard Irish protocol, the bride and groom sit in the center with the bride on the groom's left. On the groom's right is the bride's mother, the groom's father, the maid of honor, the best man, the celebrant and then the bridesmaids and groomsmen alternate. On the bride's left is the bride's father, the groom's mother, and then bridesmaids and groomsmen alternate. Also, tables are no longer confined to the oblong, banquet shape. Depending on the number of guests, many couples are now choosing round tables because they are more conducive to conversation.

FAVORS

While it isn't necessary to give every guest a memento of your wedding day, many couples like the idea, so, if the budget allows it, by all means include a small gift at each place setting. Here are a few suggestions:

After-Dinner Mints

Mint madness is how Torc Truffles of County Longford describes their dark rich creamy leaf shaped mints that melt in your mouth. Torc also offers their truffles in favor boxes which can be printed with the names of the Bride & Groom and date of the wedding. A variety of colors is available including silver, gold, navy, burgundy, green, and pink.

Chocolates

Many candy manufacturers will customize a design, but if that's too expensive for your budget, I have found two resources where you can get ready-made chocolate shamrocks, as well as the Claddagh symbol, quite reasonably priced. One of the companies also sells chocolates with an Irish cream liqueur center. Since we were on a fairly tight budget, we decided on foil-wrapped heart-shaped chocolates placed in inexpensive boxes and tied with the same ribbon used for the programs. For a unique touch, we purchased imitation wedding bands we found in an invitation catalog which we used to secure miniature scrolls. On each scroll was an Irish proverb or toast and one was placed inside each box. See Information Section IV for how to make the scrolls.

Harvest Knots

In the old days, young men braided harvest knots of straw as a symbol of their affection and intentions; the girls wore these tokens on their clothing or in their hair. You can find appropriate materials to make small harvest knots at most craft shops. Once the knots are made, you could then enhance them with tiny flowers, two imitation wedding rings, or a miniature bell. Whichever embellishment you choose, it would be a nice touch to attach a tiny scroll that explains the significance of the symbol.

Wildflower Seeds

Since marriage is a union that many couples hope will result in the growth of a family and wildflowers are so much a part of the Irish landscape, packets of Irish wildflower seeds wrapped in tissue and tied with ribbons that coordinate with your wedding colors would make for a meaningful and memorable favor.

Ornaments

One couple we know went to a craft shop and had them make ornaments based on the Claddagh symbol. You could also make ornaments yourself - a much less expensive alternative. For how to make your own salt dough ornaments, see Information Section IV.

Swan Cups

Readily available in most wedding invitation catalogs, these can be filled with candy and then wrapped in tulle, secured with a ribbon.

FOOD

From all of the research I've done into wedding celebrations in Ireland as they once were, you serve the very best food and drink you can afford. In the old days, if the bride's family was seen as stingy it could be 'thrown up to them' at a fair or festival, years later even, an embarrassment to be avoided at all costs! But that doesn't mean a family should go overboard and into debt just to look good for the neighbors. Nowadays, everyone knows that weddings can be prohibitively expensive.

According to a recent issue of *Bride's Magazine,* the cost of an average wedding has soared to around $20,000, most of which is spent on the reception. It seems like an excessive amount to spend for just several hours of entertainment. The best plan, if the bride's parents are paying for the reception, is to get a budget figure from them way ahead of time. And if you're paying for all or part of it yourselves, which many couples are doing these days, then definitely decide as soon as possible what you can comfortably manage.

The good news is that it will be a lot more like an old-fashioned Irish wedding if both families get together and share some of the responsibilities for the feast. In the old days, thoughtful relatives, friends and neighbors always brought food to their hosts so that by the time all the guests had gathered, the tables would be groaning with a huge spread which very few families could afford to put on by themselves.

Once your budget is established you can then get down to the fun of deciding what to serve. Much will depend on the size of your guest list and the formality of the celebration. It's perfectly acceptable, for example, to have everyone back to the house and offer them sandwiches, drinks, and wedding cake. For the very small reception, this is ideal. However, if you are planning a much bigger event, my best advice is to engage the services of a reputable caterer and tell them immediately that you would like to serve food reflective of your heritage. If the caterer suggests corned beef and cabbage, you might want to consider hiring someone with a little more imagination. I combed Irish cookbooks, looking for dishes that go beyond this obvious cliché.

What follows are suggestions for the feast that you can share with your caterer. Many of the dishes suggested for pre-wedding parties could also be considered. An asterisk after a dish indicates that the recipe is included in the recipe section. Note that the word 'Starter' is the equivalent of appetizer and that when planning your meal, many Irish receptions are sit-down, five-course affairs! The following are simply ideas from which to create your own menu; I'm not suggesting that you serve them all!

Soups & Starters
Leek and Potato Soup*
Malted Whiskey Liver Paté*
Dublin Prawns*
Angels on Horseback*
Irish Cheeses
Oak-Smoked Salmon
Irish Brown Bread*
White Soda Bread*
Traditional Soda Bread*
White Bread
Cream Crackers
Trenchers: These are unleavened bran loaves that were once used as trays. For a rustic country-style wedding, they would be a wonderfully authentic touch.

Salads and Vegetables
Mushroom Salad with Meade*
Spinach Salad with Mushroom Meade Vinaigrette*

Colcannon*
Boiled new potatoes*
Potatoes in their jackets
Roast potatoes
Cabbage with Parsley Sauce*

Entrées

Cold Poached Salmon
Chicken Cashel Blue*
Limerick Ham*
Leg of Lamb
Spiced Beef*
Roast Pork

Desserts/Sweets

Traditional Irish Wedding Cake*

Most wedding guests will expect dessert to be a slice of wedding cake. However, you may wish to consider offering an alternative of fresh fruits served with cream or Irish cheeses for those who would prefer something lighter.

In the old days, 'the woman of the house' would take great pride in producing the finalé for the feast. Nowadays, while most couples will use a commercial baker, you can still achieve an Irish look and flavor for your cake. Select a baker/decorator who is flexible about design and show them one or more motifs you like, such as swans, the Claddagh symbol, or even a piece of Irish lace. If you have access to it, and want to use it, the topper from the wedding cake of either the bride's parents, or the groom's would be wonderfully sentimental. The Irish love continuity and even though the topper might not reflect your Irish theme, the fact that it was used by either set of parents would make it very special.

Regardless of how your cake is decorated, whether you choose the same fresh flowers that are used in the bridesmaids' bouquets cascading down every tier or opt for a complex Irish lace design, the most important detail to remember is that the top layer should be saved for the christening celebration of your first baby. In the old days, before refrigeration, most wedding cakes would have been a fruitcake enhanced with Irish whiskey. Stored in a tin with a tight-

fitting lid, it would keep almost indefi-
nitely and improve over time. If you
decide to have at least one layer be an
Irish whiskey cake, keep in mind that
it is quite heavy and may not work if
the layers beneath it will be of a lighter
texture. Consult with your baker.
Possibly, with the excellent supports
available today, this problem can be
overcome. In any event, depending on
how many other layers you decide to
have, consider making one of them flavored with an Irish cream liqueur such
as Baileys or Carolans, or even a layer
that tastes like Irish coffee.

You might also want to think about
the old custom of hiding charms inside
one of the layers for your bridal party
to discover. I found a resource that
offers a set of charms in sterling silver.
However, they don't match the
interpretations of traditional charms
which were customarily a ring
meaning marriage within a year, a
thimble which foretold spinsterhood, a
button which meant bachelorhood, a
dried pea which signified poverty and a
coin which forecast riches. Yet another
version of this custom has the ring, a
rag, a bean, a stick and a pea. The rag
meant the person would remain single, the stick was unfortunately
associated with violence, the bean predicted poverty, and the pea
wealth. One other symbol that was often included was a little boat
which meant a journey. If you stay with tradition, these symbols are
easy to come by.

Another old Irish custom is to send pieces of cake to family and
friends unable to attend the wedding. Clearly, whether this is
feasible or not depends on what type of cake you decide to have. The

**THE HEAVENLY
BANQUET**

*I would like to have the
men of Heaven
In my own house
With vats of
good cheer
Laid out for them.
I would like to have the
three Marys
Their fame is so great.
I would like people
From every corner
of Heaven.
I would like them
to be cheerful
In their drinking.
I would like to have
Jesus too
Here amongst them.
I would like a great
lake of beer
For the King of Kings.
I would like to be
watching Heaven's family
Drinking it through
all eternity.*

same is true of the tradition where, if a single person puts a piece of cake under the bed-pillow, they will dream of their future spouse. That could be very messy if the cake is anything but a traditional Irish whiskey cake!

DRINK & BEVERAGES

To clarify the heading on this section, in my research I discovered that in Ireland, a drink means alcohol and a beverage is tea, coffee or a soft drink. It is also worth knowing that sherry is traditionally the first drink served at an Irish reception and, no, there's no such thing as a fine Irish wine made from grapes. But that doesn't mean that there are no traditional Irish wines:

Bunratty Meade or Irish Mist

Meade is the oldest drink in Ireland and no medieval banquet was complete without it. It was believed to convey powers of virility and fertility and it became the custom at weddings for the bride and groom to toast each other with special goblets full of meade which they would use for one full moon after the wedding. This tradition is the origin of the word 'honeymoon.' A brew made by Bunratty Meade is based on ancient recipes and is served at the Bunratty Castle medieval banquets. Very pleasant and easy on the palate, it is now being exported from Ireland. See the resource listing for how to contact your nearest distributor and also see the Irish Toasts below for two very special ways to thank your guests with meade. You might also be interested in knowing that Bunratty Meade now offers favor-size bottles which would make for a very nice keepsake.

Heather wine, commercially known as Irish Mist Liqueur, is like meade in that it has overtones of honey, herbs and spices. The recipe was thought to be lost until an old manuscript with the directions for making it was found in the 1940s. Daniel Williams, whose family founded the Tullamore Distillery, recognized that this was indeed the recipe for the legendary drink that was the favorite of chieftains and nobles in ancient days. Mr. Williams adapted it to create what has since become a popular after-dinner drink.

Adams Ale

This is an Irish euphemism for water. A considerate host and hostess will be sure to have pitchers of ice-water available, especially at dinner.

Sherry

It's likely that Spanish traders were the first to introduce sherry into Ireland. There are many excellent brands available and I would defer to the judgement of a good wine merchant to help you make your selection.

Cider

From plain to sparkling to "hard", it's a very popular drink in Ireland. While commercial brands are available year-round, the best is often the fresh beverage found in farmers' markets during harvest season. If you're planning a fall wedding, cider would be most appropriate.

Uisce Beatha/Water of Life/Irish Whiskey

What Irish celebration would be complete without it? The difference between Irish whiskey and Scotch whisky goes far beyond the spelling. The malt for Irish whiskey is dried in a closed kiln and not over open peat fires which give Scotch whisky its smoky flavor.

 The influence of mead was so great that the banquet hall of Tara, where the high Kings of Ireland ruled, was named the 'House of the Mead Circling.'

The difference between a porter or stout? Stout simply means strong but porter is an abbreviation for porter's ale, supposedly a weaker brew that was approved for meat market, vegetable and railway porters to drink while at work.

While it's true that Ireland can't claim a wine of the grape, until recently, home-made sloe, blackberry, elderberry, nettle, apple, rhubarb and carrot wines were common drinks.

Triple distillation and a three-year maturing period are also uniquely Irish. There are several fine whiskeys from which to choose as well as an authentic poitín (pronounced pocheen). Consumption of the home-made brew was banned in Ireland for centuries, but it is now legal, and an enterprising corporation called the Bunratty Meade and Liqueur Co., became the first to legally produce and bottle it in Ireland. Bunratty Potcheen, with its delightful changing aftertaste that sweetens as it develops, is now available for all the world to savor.

Many of the best Irish whiskey brands are also widely available, including John Power, Middleton Very Rare, Paddy, Jameson, Tullamore Dew, Bushmills, Tyrconnell single malt, Locke's and Kilbeggan, a nineteenth century brand that was re-introduced in 1994.

Beer

History tells us that in the absence of a grape-growing wine tradition, beer becomes a nation's favorite drink. It's most certainly true of Ireland! In addition to Guinness, your 'pint of plain' could include Harp Lager, Beamish stout, Smithwick's ale, as well as Kaliber, a non-alcoholic lager for the teetotalers. It's also very popular to combine a stout and lager in what's called a 'half and half.' Another festive drink is a Black Velvet which is half Guinness and half champagne.

Hot Drinks

A few centuries ago, hot drinks were all the fashion and included mulled ale, porter, punch, hot spiced wine, possets made with hot sweetened milk, spices and ale, buttered whiskey or rum, and scáiltín which was a blend of hot milk, butter, sugar and whiskey, flavored with cinnamon or cloves.

Irish Coffee*

While Irish coffee made with genuine Irish whiskey has become popular everywhere, many people are surprised to learn that it's a relatively modern invention.

The Irish Coffee story begins at Foynes Airbase in Limerick. By 1937, the base was well-established as the main airport for Flying

Boats between America and Europe. By 1940, the base was handling a large number of passengers who would often have a long wait while the Flying Boat was prepared for its next journey. Fortunately, Foynes had a restaurant which made waiting a bit less of a bother.

One winter night, in 1942, a flight left the base for Botwood, Newfoundland and then on to New York. After five grueling hours of battling a storm, the decision was made to turn back. The restaurant was informed to prepare food and drink, as the passengers would be cold and miserable.

Chef Joe Sheridan decided the passengers needed something special to warm them up. He brewed dark, rich coffee, splashed in some Irish whiskey and topped each cup off with freshly whipped cream. Supposedly, there was a hushed silence as cups were raised and the brew was tasted for the first time. "Hey Buddy," said a surprised American passenger, "is this Brazilian coffee?" "No," said Mr. Sheridan, "that's Irish Coffee."

The coffee received rave reviews. In fact, Stanton Delaplane, an international travel writer, enjoyed it so much, he brought the recipe back to Jack Koeppler, a bartender at the Buena Vista Hotel in San Francisco. They attempted to recreate it, but without success. The cool cream on top kept sinking. Mr. Koeppler returned to Ireland to learn the correct way to make it, and that led to an interesting twist on the story.

Mummers were companies of itinerant play-actors who acted at important gatherings such as fairs, weddings and wakes; in general, they were not unwelcome as they provided much amusement. However, their antics were sometimes objectionable and offensive to the families, especially at a wake if the deceased person had been unpopular, or at a wedding if there was anything unusual about the couple (an older woman marrying a young boy, for example). Sometimes the mummers came to a wedding bent on mischievous tricks and if the family found out beforehand, they'd gather together to protect themselves.
Then there was sure to be a fight.

In October 1945, as the era of the Flying Boat came to an end, Foynes Airbase closed in order to make way for more modern aircraft. A new airport was opened on the other side of the Shannon Estuary - Rineanna, which is now known as Shannon International Airport. Joe Sheridan took his famous drink to the new airport and then, in 1952, he was offered the opportunity to spread his wings. He accepted a position at the Buena Vista Hotel in San Francisco where he continued to make and introduce customers to his uniquely Irish creation comprised of cream, rich as an Irish brogue; coffee, strong as a friendly hand; sugar, sweet as the tongue of a rogue; whiskey, smooth as the wit of the land. For an authentic version of Mr. Sheridans's original drink, please see the recipe section.

Liqueurs

Since the introduction of Baileys Original Irish Cream in 1974, it has become one of the leading liqueurs in the world and accounts for a healthy percentage of all Irish exports. Its success has led to the introduction of many other cream liqueurs including Emmets, Carolans Irish Cream, St. Brendans Superior Cream Liqueur and Sheridan's, an intriguing two-part drink that comes in an unusual split-chamber glass bottle.

May God give you luck and put a good man in your way, and if he is not good, may the wedding whiskey be drunk at his wake.

What butter and whiskey won't cure, there is no cure for.

A long drink for the stranger and the best of bread and butter.
Old Brehon Law

It's customary to save a bottle of the wedding champagne for the christening celebration of the first baby, 'to wet the baby's head.' This is not a dousing of the child with the bubbly - it's an expression for a toast to the new-born.

*A Good Cup of Tea**

It may not sound terribly festive, but even in modern-day Ireland, the natives keep the kettle on at weddings, christenings, wakes, or whatever! Two brands of excellent Irish tea are Barry's from Cork and Bewley's from Dublin. See the recipe section for instructions on the traditional method of brewing a pot of tea.

IRISH TOASTS

At an Irish reception, members of the family, the wedding party and friends give speeches first, which are then followed by the traditional toasts. It might be fun to keep the champagne or Black Velvets flowing by placing one toast on each table and requesting that a guest from that table read it. Some of the ones I found are very poignant and romantic, while others are typical of the Irish spirit and sense of humor:

♣ We drink to your coffin. May it be built from the wood of a hundred year old oak tree that we shall plant tomorrow.

♣ Here's to health, peace, and prosperity. May the flower of love never be nipped by the frost of disappointment, nor shadow of grief fall among your family and friends.

♣ Wishing you always: walls for the wind, a roof for the rain, and tea by the warmth of the fire, laughter to cheer you and those you love near you, and all that your heart might desire.

♣ Slainté agus saol agat!- Health and life to you!

♣ May good luck be always your friend in all that you do, and may trouble be always a stranger to you.

♣ May your right hand always be stretched out in friendship, but never in want.

♣ May the roof above you never fall in and your friends gathered below never fall out.

♣ May the sons of your sons smile up in your face.

♣ May the Irish hills caress you, may her lakes and rivers bless you, may the luck of the Irish enfold you, may the blessings of St. Patrick behold you.

♣ May you live as long as you want, and never want as long as you live.

♣ May the saddest day of your future be no worse than the happiest day of your past.

♣ Health and long life to you, land without rent to you, a child every year to you, and if you can't go to heaven, may you die in Ireland.

♣ May there always be work for your hands to do,
May your purse always hold a coin or two,
May the sun always shine on your window pane,
May a rainbow be certain to follow each rain,
May the hand of a friend always be near you,
And may God fill your heart with gladness to cheer you.

♣ May joy and peace surround you,
Contentment latch your door,
And happiness be with you now,
And bless you ever more.

♣ May we see you grey and combing your grandchildren's hair.

♣ May you have warm words on a cold evening,
a full moon on a dark night,
and the road downhill all the way to your door.

♣ May there be a generation of children on the children of your children.

♣ May those who love us, love us, and those that don't love us, may God turn their hearts. And if He doesn't turn their hearts, may He turn their ankles, so we'll know them by their limping.

♣ May your mornings bring joy and your evenings bring peace.

♣ May your troubles grow few as your blessings increase.

♣ May your hands be forever clasped in friendship
And your hearts joined forever in love.

♣ Your lives are very special,
God has touched you in many ways.
May His blessings rest upon you
And fill all your coming days.

♣ May God in His wisdom and infinite love
Look down on you always from Heaven above.

♣ May He send you good fortune contentment and peace,
And may all your blessings forever increase!

A toast from the bride and groom to their guests

You'll need to raise glasses filled with Bunratty Meade for this special toast and the response that follows:

♣ Friends and relatives, so fond and dear,
'Tis our great pleasure to have you here.
When many years this day has passed,
Fondest memories will always last.
So we drink a cup of Irish meade,
And ask God's blessing in your hour of need.

Response from the wedding guests

♣ On this, your special day,
Our wish to you the goodness of the old,
The best of the new,
God Bless you both who drink this meade,
May it always fill your every need.

---

*There's an old tradition called 'Clootie' where guests dip pieces
of cloth into a well, make a wish for the newlyweds,
and then hang the cloth on a tree.
Contributed by Marty Shanahan*

*Mind your luggage! During the reception, the bridesmaids and best
man have been known to get access to the honeymoon suitcases
and tie all the socks and underwear together.*

MUSIC AND DANCING

As with the music for your ceremony, the possibilities for your reception are endless! While you may not want to play all Irish melodies, there's most certainly enough available to keep everyone singing and dancing for days! There are also so many choices for first dances that, unless you're really set on it, you can substitute clichés such as *Daddy's Little Girl* with Irish compositions that actually may have more meaning for you and your families. But be aware that some of the most popular tunes associated with the Emerald Isle are products of Tin Pan Alley. *When Irish Eyes Are Smiling*, for example, was actually written by George Graff, an American of Dutch and German descent. I'm not saying that you shouldn't play the old standards, especially if they are family favorites, but do check into the many recordings available that feature musicians playing traditional Irish airs and dances. You will discover a wealth of tenderness, passion and beauty that is soul-stirring.

While it's not always possible to preview a recording, amazon.com offers free sound bites which may help you avoid making the mistake of purchasing an inappropriate album which I did when I bought *A Celtic Wedding* by the Chieftains. I didn't look at the playlist. Had I done so, I would have seen immediately that all of the music is from Brittany. Yes, it's Celtic, and yes, as usual, the Chieftains are superb. But it isn't Irish.

What follows is a general chronological order of key events held during most wedding receptions. With each event, I've suggested one or two pieces. Some of the selections reference a specific artist and recording.

To set the mood, have an uilleann piper herald the arrival of the wedding party. An appropriate tune would be the recessional played at the end of your ceremony. If you are having a cocktail hour and/or receiving line prior to the meal, keep the mood going with musicians or a DJ playing traditional airs.

Arrival of the Wedding Party

Simple Gifts from the ballet Appalachian Spring by Aaron Copland. This old Shaker hymn is supposedly rooted in Celtic culture and is the theme that runs throughout Michael Flatley's *Lord of The Dance*.

Alternatively, consider *Morghan Meaghan* by Lauri Riley and Bob McNally from *Celtic Odyssey*.

Background Music

During the cocktail hour, dinner and dessert, there will be numerous opportunities to play a wide variety of Irish music. See Information Section I for ideas. When making your choices, keep in mind that you will want to encourage conversation, so it's best to select unobtrusive instrumentals and save the boisterous jigs and reels for the dancing later. Also, unless you have an excellent master of ceremonies who can time musical introductions perfectly, it's advisable not to have any music at all during the speeches and toasts.

FIRST DANCES

Bride and Groom

While many couples choose 'their song' for the first dance, *The Irish Wedding Song* by Ian Betterridge, already mentioned under Ceremony, has become almost a standard at Irish wedding receptions. It does have a lovely air and the words are beautiful. If you can play this piece during your ceremony, great, but if it's not permitted,

---

It's said that more than two thousand years ago, Druids left oak-smoked salmon as an offering to the great Dagda, god of the pagan Irish, and in the fifth century, it's believed to have been served at the banquets in Tara, seat of the high kings of Ireland.

White bread or 'shop bread' made by the town baker was always purchased for important occasions such as weddings and wakes. In some places, it was considered so indispensable when the clergy visited on 'station days' that it was also known as 'priest's bread.'

> *The potato remains a staple of Irish cuisine.*
> *The average person eats over three hundred pounds a year.*
>
> *A trout in the pot is better than a salmon in the sea.*
>
> *My tastes are very simple. The best is good enough for me.*
> OSCAR WILDE

it may be appropriate for your first dance together. If you select it, do be sure to have copies of the lyrics available so that all of your guests can sing it to you. An excellent version is *The Irish Wedding Song* by Andy Cooney from *A Collection of Irish Hits.*

Father and Daughter
Daughter of Mine by John McDermott from *Love is a Voyage*
Fairy Tale by Eyna from *The Celts*
Sure, She's Irish by Sonny Knowles from *Sunshine & Shamrocks*

Mother and Son
Did Your Mother Come From Ireland by Bing Crosby from *Shamrocks & Shillelaghs.* It's also on his *Top O' The Morning* recording.

Parents
Voyage by Christy Moore from *The Christy Moore Collection.*
This is a splendid tribute to marriage as are *The Vows go Unbroken* and *My Little Claddagh Ring* by Andy Cooney from his *Collection of Irish Hits.*

Bridesmaids and Groomsmen
Mari's Wedding by Van Morrison and The Chieftains from *Irish Heartbeat.* Actually a Scottish melody, but it's so popular and full of joy, it merits inclusion.

SPECIAL EVENTS

Cake Cutting
Air - You're The One by the Chieftain's from *Film Cuts.*
A Stór mó Chroí - Jewel of My Heart by Maura O'Connell from *Wandering Home.*

Bouquet and Garter Toss

The Humour Is On Me Now, a jaunty Irish tune played at the reception in the movie, *The Quiet Man*. The soundtrack is available.

GENERAL DANCING

Before getting into the wild jigs and reels and perhaps a few sets featuring contemporary Irish musicians, consider beginning the general dancing with *Happy Are We All Together* by Andy Cooney, a lovely ballad in a traditional slow waltz tempo. It's on his *Collection of Irish Hits*.

LAST DANCE

Instead of the traditional send-off, complete with old shoes and tin cans tied to the bumper of the getaway car, many couples are staying until the end of their reception because they don't want to miss out on any of the fun. And why not! If you plan to stay until the end, consider leading your guests out of the reception hall to a lively jig such as *Up and About* from the album *James Galway and the The Chieftains in Ireland*. It's recorded live and you can clearly hear the hard shoes of Irish dancers, which, by the way, would also be a wonderful addition to your reception. Consider inviting several dancers to do a soft shoe and hard shoe set during the dinner hour. While they are changing shoes, perhaps one of the dancers can explain the significance of their magnificent costumes. For your guests who may never have watched Irish dancing before, it could be a major highlight of the celebration!

Note: For companies, products or services mentioned in this chapter, please consult:

The Resource Listing in Section VI
The North American Celtic Buyers Association website.
If you live in the United States or Canada, they have a great search function that will enable you to find the nearest Irish shop:
www.celticbuyers.com
My website:
www.irishcultureandcustoms.com/Weddings/WeddingRsrcs.html

7

THE SCATTERING
POST-WEDDING PARTIES

Traditionally, the Irish celebrated three stages of an event: the Gathering, the Day and the Scattering. The Gathering celebrates the coming together of family and friends, the Day is devoted to the celebration of anything from local saints and marriages to sporting events and folk rituals, and the Scattering celebrates the parting of the guests.

With the exception of a traditional Irish breakfast, many of the activities and menu suggestions already mentioned in previous sections would be appropriate for the Scattering. Even if you have already left for your honeymoon, you can arrange with your parents to host, on your behalf, a brunch, lunch, high tea or dinner. And if, as with many newlyweds nowadays, you're not leaving on your honeymoon right away, then you can join with families and friends for one more round of festivities. Either way, the day after is a great opportunity for people to share memories while they are still fresh and, if you do plan to be there, it might also be an appropriate time to open the wedding gifts received at your reception.

About the only meal we haven't covered in this book so far is breakfast. And when it comes to one that is traditionally Irish, there are many who may think I've saved the best for last. An old-fashioned breakfast in Ireland was a robust meal which would give rural folk the energy required to toil long and hard. A side benefit that we discovered while we were there, was gaining the stamina to walk great distances.

While you'll find fresh fruit as well as granola, muesli and other cereals on today's Irish breakfast table, the traditional menu includes: Irish bacon, Irish pork sausages, black pudding, white pudding, eggs, tomato, toast, soda bread, marmalade, orange juice and coffee or tea. Even if you don't live in Ireland, nowadays it's possible to have *genuine* Irish ingredients delivered right to your door!

Many people like to embellish these core ingredients with fried mushrooms and you might also want to consider an Ulster Fry which would include fadge,* a fried potato bread, or boxty,* a potato pancake that is a specialty of the northwestern part of Ireland. As Padraig Óg Gallagher of Gallagher's Boxty House in Dublin put it, "There are as many recipes for boxty as there are parishes in Leitrim." Yet another staple of the Irish breakfast table is porridge made from old fashioned steel-cut Irish oats. McCann's is a popular brand.

If your reception carries on into the wee hours, your family and guests may want to sleep in and skip breakfast altogether. In that case, consider putting on a Ploughman's Lunch as described under stag parties, or perhaps an afternoon tea similar to what was suggested for hen parties. Whatever you decide to do, the idea is to 'scatter' your people well-fed, contented, and with fond memories of incomparable Irish hospitality.

If a newly married woman hadn't moved to her new home before Lent begian, she would have to stay where she was until Easter. The night she actually moved, her husband and a small group would come to meet her on the road. Similarly, there would be a small group of the wife's relatives setting out to accompany her to her new dwelling. When they met, the two groups stayed with the wife and as soon as she was inside the house, her mother-in-law would stand before her in the middle of the floor. She would then remove the cloak from the young woman's shoulders, take her by both hands and say: 'Wisha (husband's last name) welcome to you, a welcome and forty to you all, and may the young pair have seven sons.'
FROM *THE MAN FROM CAPE CLEAR*, CONCHÚR Ó SIOCHÁIN

BLESSINGS

If you have all gathered with the happy couple, there may be an appropriate moment to use one of the following traditional blessings:

♣ May May the road rise to meet you
May the wind always be at your back
May the sun shine warm on your face
the rains fall soft upon your fields until we meet again,
may God hold you in the palm of his hand.

♣ The health of the salmon to you,
Deep peace of the running wave to you,
Deep peace of the flowing air to you,
Deep peace of the quiet earth to you,
Deep peace of the shining stars to you,
Deep peace of the watching shepherds to you,
Deep peace of the Son of Peace to you.

♣ Bless you and yours as well as the cottage you live in. May the roof overhead be well-thatched, and those inside well matched.

♣ A parent's blessing on a son or daughter leaving home
The great God between your two shoulder blades
To protect you in your going and returning,
The Son of the Virgin Mary be close to your heart,
And the perfect Holy Spirit be keeping an eye on you.

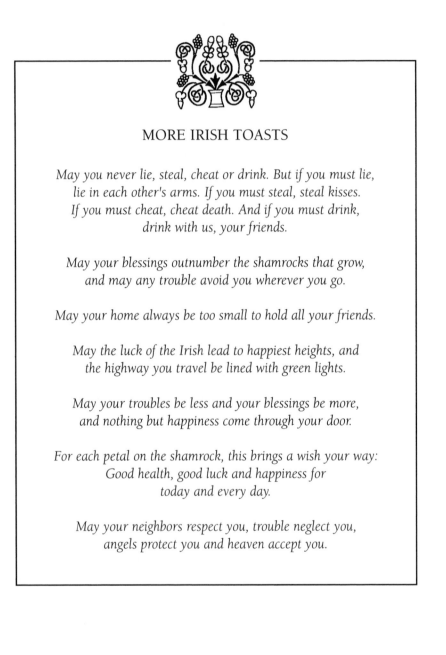

MORE IRISH TOASTS

May you never lie, steal, cheat or drink. But if you must lie,
lie in each other's arms. If you must steal, steal kisses.
If you must cheat, cheat death. And if you must drink,
drink with us, your friends.

May your blessings outnumber the shamrocks that grow,
and may any trouble avoid you wherever you go.

May your home always be too small to hold all your friends.

May the luck of the Irish lead to happiest heights, and
the highway you travel be lined with green lights.

May your troubles be less and your blessings be more,
and nothing but happiness come through your door.

For each petal on the shamrock, this brings a wish your way:
Good health, good luck and happiness for
today and every day.

May your neighbors respect you, trouble neglect you,
angels protect you and heaven accept you.

POST WEDDING CUSTOMS

Before leaving the subject of post-wedding parties, I should mention three other traditions which offer the opportunity for gathering family and friends together. The first Sunday after the wedding was known as Bride's Sunday and friends who had been invited to the previous week's festivities accompanied the newly-married couple to chapel. The young couple were then further honored by being invited to the bridesmaid's house for tea or dinner. Another custom that was strictly adhered to was not allowing a bride to enter her old home for any reason until 30 days after the marriage. This probably evolved from the notion that she needed time to recover from any homesickness she might be feeling; it would also allow her time to settle into her new residence. On the 30th night after the wedding, a big party and dance were arranged by her parents to welcome their daughter and her new husband for a visit. This celebration was known as the 'hauling home.'

A third tradition took place on the first May-day after the wedding. The young people of the parish went to the woods and cut down the tallest tree they could find. They then trimmed it with ribbons, colored paper and other decorations and carried it to the newlywed's house where they set it up in front of the door. With the fiddlers playing a joyful jig, the young men and women danced around the tree with hands joined together, separating only to welcome the newlyweds into the circle.

If my research has proven anything, it's something I already knew. We Irish love to enjoy ourselves and will use just about any excuse to get together for an evening of story-telling, music, singing and dancing. True, a wedding was always a major event, but so were wakes, christenings, confirmations, festivals, fairs, harvests and literally hundreds of other reasons for revelry. Fodder for another book? Perhaps. In the meantime, I hope this one will help you plan a celebration that will make you even more proud of your Irish heritage.

Note: For companies, products or services mentioned in this chapter, please consult:

The Resource Listing in Section VI
The North American Celtic Buyers Association website.
If you live in the United States or Canada, they have a great search function that will enable you to find the nearest Irish shop:
www.celticbuyers.com
My website:
www.irishcultureandcustoms.com/Weddings/WeddingRsrcs.html

8

OH, IRELAND ISN'T IT GRAND YOU LOOK
A HONEYMOON IN IRELAND

At 32,637 square miles, including the North and the Republic, 'The Realm of Romance' is slightly larger than West Virginia in the USA and smaller than the state of Ohio. But for such a tiny place, Ireland is a magnificent, multifaceted gem, blessed with an abundance of details and differences. Majestic mountains sweep down to the sea. Miles of stone walls line fields filled with black-faced sheep. Tall, flowering hedges shade narrow, winding roads. Ancient castles and mystical abbeys dominate pastoral vistas. Pastel-hued cottages dot river valleys strewn with wild flowers. What a magical place to begin married life together!

In this section, you'll find information about different types of honeymoons, places to stay, practical tips from our daughter, who is an experienced international travel counselor, the honeymoon memories of a dear friend, driving tips and a suggested basic itinerary by Weddings on the Move, a company that specializes in arranging international weddings and honeymoons. Bord Fáilte, the Irish Tourist Board for the Republic of Ireland, and the Northern Irish Tourist Board are worth contacting as they are both most helpful. Of great value in learning about Ireland is the publication *Ireland of the Welcomes*, published by Bord Fáilte. It's a bi-monthly magazine filled with articles and features on people, places, restaurants and cultural attractions. Bord Fáilte also offers a free Irish vacation kit. To subscribe to the magazine or receive the kit, see the resource listing where you'll find phone numbers and addresses for the tourist boards, other Irish publications and the travel-related companies mentioned in this section, including Weddings on the Move.

CHOOSING THE PERFECT HONEYMOON

Most couples honeymooning in Ireland fall into three categories. Many go to visit relatives. Others find a romantic spot and stay there for the entire time. Still others try to see as much as possible. Probably the best tip I can give to people who have never been there is to slow down and take it easy. Irish time is very different from most countries and it's one of the biggest reasons people find the place so enchanting. Stop to ask for directions and you could well be engaged in a dialog similar to: "You see that road over there, well, don't take that one." Drop into a pub for lunch and the locals seem to know exactly when you want to become a part of the conversation and also when you'd rather be left to yourselves. But no matter which, you'll always hear "safe journey" on your way out the door.

Whether or not you fall into one of the three categories already mentioned, when you begin deciding on what type of honeymoon you'd prefer, you might want to consider one or more of the following:

Ancestral Journey

If you're both of Irish descent, perhaps you could begin your honeymoon in the county where the bride's family is from and end it in the ancestral home of the groom, or vice versa. Naturally, if you still have relatives living in either or both counties, you'll want let them know you're coming so you can arrange a visit. You'll never hear the end of it if you don't drop by for a cup of tea.

They got married, a made match, and they made history,
for they were the first couple from that part of the world
to go away on a honeymoon. When they got off the train
above in Glanmire Station in Cork, she says to him:
'They are all looking at us. They know very well that we are
fresh from the altar! Is there anything I could do,' says she,
'to make it appear as if we are a couple of years married?'
'Of course there is,' he said. 'Catch hold of the bag
and walk on in front of me!'

Killary Tours

This company is situated on the shores of Killary Harbor in Leenane, County Galway. If you like the great outdoors, Killary Tours may have just what you're looking for. They specialize in active honeymoon packages, including self-guided cycling and hiking tours. Or you can opt to stay at Killary Lodge and try your hand at sailing a catamaran, canoeing, kayaking, horse-back riding, scuba diving or teasing each other on the High Ropes course. One couple particularly enjoyed their self-guided tour through Connemara because they weren't among the countless other newlyweds one usually finds at popular honeymoon resorts. Love the idea of sailing on the high seas? Killary can arrange for a cruise on an authentic Galway hooker - a fishing boat distinguished by its red sails and a history that spans centuries. For a very reasonable sum, you'll have a skipper, a cook, and plenty of time to sample a taste of Ireland that very few people have ever experienced. And if you're interested in having your ceremony take place in Ireland, Killary can make all of the arrangements. The lodge is a charming country house offering 20 bedrooms (each with its own bathroom), excellent home-cooked food, extensive wine list, tennis court, sauna and all of the warm hospitality one expects of the Irish. There's even a stone chapel located nearby which is owned by a professional wedding photographer.

Oideas Gaelic Language Center, County Donegal

While surfing the net, I found Lynn and Eamon Callaly, who used to run an Irish matchmaking business. They put me in contact with Liam Ó Cuinneagáin who has earned quite a reputation for matchmaking himself. As many as four or five weddings take place each year between couples who met while participating in one of the center's courses. I'm not surprised. Both the locations in southwest Donegal - one on the scenically splendid Sliabh Liag peninsula and the other on the fringe of the impressive Blue Stack Mountains - are in a Gaeltacht region renowned for the richness of its traditional culture, its music, story-telling and prehistoric settlements. Founded in 1984 to promote the learning and use of the Irish language and to foster Irish culture, the center offers the opportunity to participate in everyday Gaeltacht life. So, if you'd like

In doggerel and stout let us honour this country,
though the air is so soft that it smudges the words.
LOUIS MACNIECE

Dear Erin, how sweetly thy green bosom rises!
An emerald set in the ring of the sea.
JOHN PHILPOT CURRAN

Erin, the tear and the smile in thine eyes
blend like the rainbow that hangs in the skies.
THOMAS MOORE

to learn how to say I love you in Gaelic, this is definitely the place to go. You can spend a weekend taking courses that range from hill-walking to tapestry weaving, or you can become immersed in the language and culture through intensive two-week study programs.

Shannon and Erne River Cruises

With the restoration of the 40-mile link between the Shannon and the Erne in 1994, Ireland's two great waterways have been joined to form a magnificent chain of lakes and rivers stretching from Beleek in County Fermanagh to Killaloe in County Clare, a distance of almost 300 miles. You can cruise these spectacular waters on barges accommodating from two to 22 guests. Or you can rent a self-drive cruiser (boat) and explore the rivers on your own. To arrange one of these uniquely different vacations, check with your travel agent or you can contact one of the two companies I found who specialize in voyages on Ireland's inland waterways. More interested in a cruise to a tropical destination but one with a totally Irish atmosphere? Then check out Irish Festival Cruises which, along with all of the above, can be found in the resource listing or on my website.

PLACES TO STAY

Choosing the perfect hotel or guest house couldn't be simpler than it is in Ireland. Just look for the Shamrock Quality Symbol. This distinctive symbol is given by the Irish Tourist Board only to those hotels, guesthouses and B&Bs which have met its exacting high standards of excellence in accommodations and service. It's your guarantee of quality. Best of all, because most of these places are family-owned and managed, you'll feel as if you are being welcomed into their home. Warmth, hospitality, and friendliness are trademarks of Irish accommodations.

Irish Hotels

The Irish hotel is unique in that it is often the social center of the community and they'll offer you much more than a bed and a meal. Many are fully-fledged leisure, business and community centers with every imaginable facility and amenity, providing food, accommodations, sports, entertainment and other attractions. If your honeymoon involves touring the country as opposed to staying in one place, the *Be Our Guest* guide published by the Irish Hotels Federation will be very helpful in selecting your next place to stay. The guide is available through the Irish Tourist Board, or you can get one from your travel agent.

Guest Houses and B&Bs

A listing of Irish Tourist Board approved places is published by Town and Country Homes Association. Within its nearly 400 pages, you'll find accommodations that range from tiny thatched cottages to magnificent ocean-front mansions. It was in this book that we found Mandalay, a beautiful B&B overlooking an inlet of Galway Bay. Our room had a balcony from which we could watch the sun go down (yes, just as in the ballad) and in the morning, when the tide was out, we could see groups of riders from a nearby stable cantering their horses across the sands. Utterly romantic!

Historic Private Homes

For a unique departure from conventional accommodations, consider contacting The Hidden Ireland, a company that represents

O Ireland, isn't it grand you look -
Like a bride in her rich adornin' ?
And with all the pent-up love of my heart
I bid you top of the mornin'! John Locke

O, Ireland! O, Ireland! We're never far apart
For you and all your beauty fill my mind and touch my heart.

Land of heart's desire,
Where beauty has no ebb, decay no flood
But joy is wisdom, time an endless song.

a collection of private houses all over Ireland. Some are great houses, at the center of large estates. Several have been designed by famous architects and lived in or visited by famous people. Others are smaller, but no less beautiful or interesting. All are surrounded by their own tree-studded parks or by gardens, often internationally renowned. And all are in the most scenic or historic areas.

Magnificent Castles and Manors

Isle Inn Tours can arrange a stunning array of castle accommodations in a special honeymoon program that's available year round. Depending on how long you will be staying and where you would like to go, Isle Inn will customize an itinerary that will take you to some of Ireland's most famous castles: Ashford, Dromoland, Waterford, Kilkea, Cabra and Castle Leslie; or to spectacular manor houses such as Adare or Hayfield. A few years ago, they also began arranging stays at St. Cleran's Manor in County Galway. It was formerly the home of film director John Huston, who once described it as "the most beautiful house in all of Ireland." Isle Inn can also arrange stays at many other deluxe properties. Think you can't afford to stay in a castle? You may be surprised to learn that it's not as costly as you might expect and you can also combine castle stays with other accommodations to make your trip more affordable. Check with Isle Inn or your travel agent to see what's available.

From Friendly Homes to Havens and Hideaways

Adams and Butler, a company based in Dublin, offers a wide range of options. For example, The Friendly Homes of Ireland is a collection of private country houses, country inns and family run hotels offering the real Ireland, well away from the tour buses. You can experience the best of Irish culture and life "far from the madding crowd". Their Havens & Hideaways also offers a great many choices, from quaint cottages to unique villas, city apartments to penthouses, stately mansions to luxury castles. You can select from more than 800 vacation rentals they describe as perfect for honeymoons.

ॐ

SOME FAVORITE SIGHTS

While few of us will ever have the luxury of spending a six-month honeymoon in Ireland (or anywhere, for that matter) that's exactly what Lynn and Eamon Callaly did a couple of years ago. In fact, their goal to make mad, passionate love in every one of the 32 counties was picked up by the Irish newspapers. Did they succeed in realizing their objective? I'll never tell! Realistically, most couples honeymooning in Ireland will stay for about ten days. Depending on where your itinerary takes you, if any of the following are close by, they're worth including:

Kylemore Abbey, County Galway

Situated near Letterfrack, its hauntingly beautiful setting is one of the most photographed locations in the country.

The Sky Road out of Clifden, County Galway

Hairpin turns, sheep in the road, ocean views and mountain vistas - you'll see them all!

The Cliffs of Moher, County Clare

Located three miles west of Liscannor, they say that if you stand at the top on a breezy afternoon you can lean back against the wind - and you won't fall down. I take no responsibility for calm days or daredevils! Five miles long and 700 feet high, these magnificent cliffs are home to thousands of birds - but bring binoculars if you really want to get a close look at them.

The Rock of Cashel, County Tipperary

One of the most spectacular archeological sites in Ireland, mighty stone walls encircle a complete round tower, a roofless abbey, a 12th century Romanesque chapel, and numerous other buildings and high crosses. This is also where Brian Boru was crowned King of Munster.

Garinish Island, County Cork

The island is in Bantry Bay, Glengariff and you reach it by ferry. For a very small admission charge, you can explore one of the most beautiful gardens in the world. On the way to and from the island, you may also see seals basking on rocks jutting out of the bay.

The Beara Way, County Cork

We loved West Cork and this peninsula is one of the reasons. The locals told us that it was just as breathtaking as the Ring of Kerry, but we wouldn't run into tons of tourist buses. It was, and we didn't.

The Dingle Peninsula, County Kerry

A spectacular region, especially the Connor Pass. Whether you're looking toward Tralee or back toward Dingle, the views are astonishing.

I could list dozens more, but a honeymoon is a very personal matter and no doubt, you'll have your own ideas about where to go and what to see. I can say with confidence, however, that what ever you do decide to do, you won't be disappointed.

PRACTICAL TRAVEL TIPS

I recommend that you make your travel plans through a certified and well-travelled counselor. Preferably, find someone who has been to Ireland and can make suggestions based on personal experience. At the very least, your counselor should be thoroughly experienced with booking international trips. By being very selective in choosing your travel agent, you'll receive better service and information. Most important of all, when you put your travel arrangements in experienced hands, you'll have one less thing to worry about during those hectic weeks before the wedding.

Because most honeymoon couples prefer to be by themselves, you won't find many of them taking an escorted tour. Independent travel is far and away the most popular choice for new-lyweds. They can come and go as they please, with no restrictions as to schedules and stops. While that level of flexibility is very appealing, I urge you to have your travel agent arrange for confirmed accommodations on your first night, especially if you'll be traveling during the months of June, July and August. That is high season in Ireland and many of the most desirable properties will be fully booked. This same advice also applies to car rentals. If you plan to hire a car, make the arrangements in advance.

The best time to visit the Emerald Isle? For lower prices, fewer tourists, and surprisingly mild weather, go between September and May. But even during the summer months, don't expect consistent blue skies and sunshine. Year-round, it's breezy and often rainy. Some regions have a drier climate than others, but most areas experience a daily dose of what the Irish euphemistically call 'soft weather'. Bring good-quality waterproof jackets and just enjoy what gives this little bit of heaven its forty shades of green.

CONTRIBUTED BY CATHERINE HAGGERTY

A BASIC ITINERARY

The following information is contributed by Weddings on the Move, a company based in the United States and comprised of travel professionals who are thoroughly familiar with a chosen destination. Ireland is one of their favorites! This itinerary incorporates many of the most popular places to visit:

Day 1:   Depart from the United States for an overnight flight to Dublin.

Day 2:   You will be met at the airport for your private transfer to your hotel or B&B. Spend the day at your leisure.

Day 3:   Enjoy a day of sightseeing in Dublin. Visit St. Patrick's Cathedral, see Georgian homes and perhaps the Book of Kells at Trinity College, as well as many other historic public buildings.

Day 4:   Rent a car or hire a private car and driver to take you to Waterford. Tour the famous Waterford Crystal factory. Enjoy the rest of the day shopping and sightseeing.

Day 5:   Drive along the south coast to Blarney Castle and kiss the renowned 'stone of eloquence.' Pick up some bargains at Blarney Woolen Mills before heading up the coast to Killarney. Enjoy breathtaking scenery and in the evening, make a few stops at the region's famous singing pubs.

Day 6:   Drive to Limerick and spend the afternoon at Bunratty Folk Park. That evening, relish the entertainment and authentic food of a genuine medieval banquet held in the 15th-century Bunratty Castle.

Day 7:   Take a full day to experience the renowned Ring of Kerry and see some of the most spectacular scenery in Ireland.

Day 8:   Depart Killarney and take the ferry across the River Shannon, the longest river in the country. Drive to the dramatic Cliffs of Moher and then on to the cosmopolitan city of Galway.

Day 9:   Drive back to Dublin for an extra night stay. Enjoy an evening at leisure.

Day 10:   Depart Dublin for your flight back to the United States. Once a booking has been made, this basic itinerary can be customized to match your budget and the time you have available. The ultimate goal of Weddings on the Move is to make your honeymoon in Ireland an unforgettable once-in-a-life-time experience.

BLESSINGS FOR A JOURNEY

May the strength of three be in your journey.

Going over the deep place, O God of patience, take them by the hand.
In case of a blow from a strong wave, O Mary,
look out for them and don't leave them.

DRIVING TIPS

Any travel is a combination of fun and aggravation. A trip to Ireland is no different. Your itinerary is easy enough and the hospitality is all you can want but, unless you are on a tour bus or plan on spending your entire time in town, the only practical way to see the countryside is to put on your hiking boots... or rent a car.

On arrival at either Dublin or Shannon airport, you're likely to have jet lag. To fully recover from the flight and enjoy a more relaxing first day, I would suggest that you have your travel agent arrange for you to pick up your rental car the next day and hire a limousine or taxi to take you to your B&B or hotel.

When you are ready to hit the road, you'll find that all of the major car rental agencies have offices at the airports and in the cities. This means that if you want to pick up your car in one location and drop it off at a different one, you should be able to do so without incurring a drop-off charge. But do check to make sure. Also, keep in mind that automatics are the most popular and they are usually the first out the door. So, while your travel agent may have specified an automatic, there's no guarantee that one will be waiting for you. If you can't drive a stick shift, you may be waiting around for an automatic to be returned.

Once you're set to go, always remember that you'll be driving on the left and sitting on the right. Now, for all of you who have never driven on the left, you must burn two life-saving truths into your brain: first, always look to the right. That's where the traffic is coming from. And second, when you turn onto (or off of) any road, you are turning into the left lane. This may seem obvious, but it's not. The most common mistake is turning right into the right lane. Some travelers find it useful to put a sign up on the dashboard saying DRIVE ON THE LEFT! Great idea, that, because it will be a constant reminder whenever you're in the car.

Driving from the airport or out of the city will most likely bring you to and through one or more roundabouts. They are a brilliant solution to the problem of intersecting roads and consist of a largish circular mound with multiple roadways entering from the perimeter. No traffic lights. No police. You enter the circle and drive around (and around and around) until you find the other road you want. Then you exit. There are rules involved. The first and foremost is: the car on the right has the right of way. This means the vehicle already on the roundabout (going around in the circle) has the right of way. Having given way you enter the roundabout and if you are going to pass more than one other road off the circle, you move to the inside lane. Begin indicating your intention to leave the circle at the road before the one at which you wish to exit. Although it sounds complicated, believe it or not, roundabouts can actually be fun.

The main roads in Ireland are designated by 'N' (National) with a number, and the signs to wherever you're going are usually clear and obvious. However, since Ireland's road system is currently going through major improvements, you'd be wise to invest in a good, recently published road map. The speed limits are marked and if not, the national speed limit is 60 miles per hour. I can't say the Irish pay much attention, they seem to drive as fast as they can! Also, as in many countries nowadays, there is a seatbelt law in effect; adults must 'fasten up' and if you are driving with children under twelve, they're not allowed to sit in the front passenger seat.

Between any major cities, Shannon Airport near Limerick and Galway City, for example, the roads are mostly good - smooth and wide. But, they're never consistent. You can expect a variation from narrow two-lane blacktop to routes that resemble American highways. Many of the good roads are four-lane, but you should only use the center two. The other two lanes (on the outer edges) are for very slow vehicles. Be prepared. I never drove anywhere without seeing, or more painfully, following, a massive tractor grinding along at about 20 miles an hour. They are always just around the next bend (out if sight) and you are going 50. Or were!

Did I say the roads were clearly marked? Well, yes, on the nice bits. On the narrow lanes, however, the signs are usually obscured by very attractive greenery. I learned to scan the brush for a hint of metal signpost. It's all part of a driving experience that forces visitors, at least, to slow down. It makes you wonder whether 'life in the slow lane' wasn't coined just for the Emerald Isle, with at least a partial tongue in cheek! There are many other rules and conventions I could share with you, but it will be more fun for you to discover them for yourself. Although it may sound daunting, Ireland is easier to drive in than most urban areas and more to the point, it's a wonderful place full of wonderful people. So go. Drive. And be not afraid.

CONTRIBUTED BY RUSS HAGGERTY

As the green hills are drenched with rain drops
Like a mother's tears of joy when her child comes home from the sea,
So does my heart weep when we are sometimes parted, you from me.
Therefore, let us make this pact, to let love bind us, one to another,
To always return, 'ere the green hills' grasses turn brown.
May we live in peace without weeping,
May our joy outline the lives we touch without ceasing,
And, may our love fill the world, angel wings tenderly beating.

HONEYMOON MEMORIES

My husband made no plans other than to buy the plane tickets. I still remember the wonderful spiral landing at Shannon and the glorious green of the fields as we came through the clouds. We rented a car, bought a good map, a booklet of B&Bs and off we went. We charted our route each evening and got off to an early start the next day. We visited Lawrence's relatives in Ballina, County Mayo - actually stayed in the same cottage in which his father was born and raised, toured the Lakes of Killarney, kissed the Blarney Stone in Cork, fell in love with Irish Soda Bread - and got lost in Dublin.

We arrived in Dublin at midnight with no place to stay and since it was a week night, couldn't find anything open. Lawrence was a firefighter, so we drove to the fire station to see if they could suggest where we might go. They recommended Mrs. Fagan. A lovely woman, they said, who supplemented her widow's pension by taking in travelers. And would she take us in at such a late hour? A quick phone call confirmed that Mrs. Fagan would leave the light on. On our way to her home in Howth we got lost and stopped a young man out for a walk. "Would ye be Yanks now?" he said, "I'll just hop in and direct you." What a grand fellow! He insisted that it was no trouble and he'd enjoy the walk home. Mrs. Fagan turned out to be just as the Dublin firefighters described her. She welcomed us warmly and treated us like family. Everywhere we went, we ran into people like her and the young man who gave us directions. Wouldn't it be wonderful if the whole world were like that? When we returned home, I thought that if we ever went back to Ireland, we'd make better plans. But unplanned really worked - we weren't held to any schedule and I'd do it all over again in just that way.

CONTRIBUTED BY JUDITH & LAWRENCE FLYNN,
MAYFIELD, OHIO

Note: For companies, products or services mentioned in this chapter, please consult:

The Resource Listing in Section VI

The North American Celtic Buyers Association website.

If you live in the United States or Canada, they have a great search function that will enable you to find the nearest Irish shop:

www.celticbuyers.com

My website:

www.irishcultureandcustoms.com/Weddings/WeddingRsrcs.html

INFORMATION AND RESOURCES

I

MUSIC

In this section, you'll find music suggestions in addition to those already mentioned within the main body of the book. Selections are listed by appropriateness to specific parts of the wedding ceremony and key events at the reception. When we began choosing our compositions, we added a great number of new CDs and cassette tapes to our already quite extensive Celtic music collection. We also checked out recordings from our public library. We then spent many very pleasurable hours listening to every recording and choosing our favorite pieces. These were written down on separate lists - one for the ceremony and one for the reception. In addition to the title of the cut and the cassette or CD from which it came, we included the length of each recording. This made it a lot easier to calculate how many pieces could be used, and it is absolutely essential if you'll be playing pre-recorded music. For example, the music played before the ceremony begins usually lasts for about a half hour.

The most difficult part of the task will be limiting your lists! Once you have made your final choices, I suggest that you dub them onto cassette tapes in the order they will be be played - ceremony on one side and reception on the other. Alternatively, if you have access to a CD burner, you could burn one CD for the ceremony and one for the reception. If you will be using a sound system at the church and reception, make a tape or CD for each location and, as a precautionary measure, make two more copies as back-ups. You should then give or mail the tapes to the people who will be responsible for running the sound system. On the big day, be certain to have someone bring the back-ups to both the ceremony and reception... just in case!

If you are engaging the services of church music directors and/or musicians, send a copy of your music to both parties prior to meeting with them, so that they will be familiar with the compositions you have selected. In turn, if you decide to use a composition suggested by your music director, he or she should provide your musicians with copies of the sheet music.

If all of this sounds incredibly time-consuming, it is! Allow about three months to make your choices and also take into consideration rehearsal time for the musicians. It will be well worth the effort.

All of the following compositions appear on recordings that are readily available. I have also included the name of the artist and the recording. Many of these compositions have been recorded by more than one artist; the ones listed here are from our personal collection. I have also offered multiple suggestions for each part of the ceremony. In segments where normally only one piece is played, the first composition listed is what was selected for our daughter's wedding. This also applies to key events held during the reception.

CEREMONY

Prelude

Carolan's Welcome. Derek Bell, Carolan's Favorites
Madame Cole. The Chieftains, Celtic Harp. This piece was composed by Carolan in 1719 for Madame Cole's wedding day.
Love Theme from Tristan & Isolde. The Chieftains, Film Cuts
Carolan's Ramble to Cashel. Northern Lights, Celtic Odyssey
Women of Ireland. Sunita, Mist-covered Mountains
Slumbering Minstrel. Nancy Bick Clarke/Sara Johnson, Crossing to Ireland
Barry Lyndon, Love Theme. The Chieftains, Film Cuts
Neansaí Mhíle Grá. Clannad, A Celtic Tapestry
An Chuilfhionn. DruidStone, The Vow - An Irish Wedding Celebration
Celtic Melody. DruidStone, The Vow - An Irish Wedding Celebration

Mothers' Seating & Candle Lighting

In traditional Irish weddings, the mothers of the bride and groom are usually escorted to their pew by an usher. In a departure from tradition, you may wish to consider having the mothers be escorted to the altar on either side of the groom. He waits for them while they light the candles on either side of the Unity candle and then he escorts them to their seats. If you decide to include this in your ceremony, one of the following compositions would be appropriate.
Believe Me If All Those Endearing Young Charms. James Galway/Phil Coulter, Legends
An Irish Lullaby. Frank Patterson, Ireland's Best Loved Ballads
Silver Threads Among The Gold. Phil Coulter, Sea of Tranquility
Irish Meditation II. El McQueen, A Celtic Tapestry
Connemara Cradle Song. Frank Patterson, Love Songs of Ireland

Processional

Bridesmaids:
Circle of Friends/Air - You're The One. The Chieftains, *Film Cuts*
March of the King of Laoise. Sunita, *Mist-Covered Mountains*
Fanny Power. James Galway and the Chieftains in Ireland.
This would also make a great processional for the bride.
Bride:
Lark In The Clear Air. James Galway, title cut of the CD
Processional. DruidStone, *The Vow - An Irish Wedding Celebration*
The Pearl. Silly Wizard, *A Celtic Tapestry*

Unity Candle

Give Me Your Hand. James Galway & The Chieftains in Ireland
Eleanor Plunkett. Deanta, *A Celtic Treasure, The Legacy of Turlough
O'Carolan*
Sí Bheag, Sí Mhór. Phil Coulter, *A Celtic Treasure, The Legacy of Turlough
O'Carolan*
Mabel Kelly. James Galway & The Chieftains in Ireland
Alleluia. James Galway & The Chieftains in Ireland

Communion

Be Thou My Vision. Celtic Hymns. We used a wedding text called *God
In The Planning* from the Gather Hymnal published by Gia
Publication, Inc. Chicago.
Bí, a Íosa, im Cróise is a beautiful traditional piece that means Oh
Jesus Every Moment.
Sweet Sacrament Divine. Various artists, *Faith of Our Fathers II*

Flowers To The Blessed Virgin

I Sing A Maid. Toot Sweet, *Celtic Christmas*
Oh Mary of Graces. Dennis and Paula Doyle, *The Contemplative Celt*
Salve Regina. Various artists. *Faith of Our Fathers I*
Ave Maria. James Galway, *Christmas Carol*
Holy Mary Full of Grace. Various artists, *Faith of Our Fathers II*

Meditation

The King Of Love My Shepherd Is. Celtic Hymns
Traditional Irish Hymn Suite. Various artists. *Faith of Our Fathers II*
Hail Glorious St. Patrick. Dennis and Paula Doyle, *The Contemplative Celt*

Recessional

Morghan Meaghan. Riley & Bob McNally, *Celtic Odyssey*
Haste to the Wedding. DruidStone, *The Vow*
Bridget Cruise. Dominig Bouchaud & Cyrille Colas, *Celtic Treasure, the Legacy of Turlough O'Carolan*
The Merry Quaker. Celtic Hymns
Tribute To Bunting. The Chieftains, *Celtic Harp*
Carolan's Concerto. James Galway & The Chieftains In Ireland

RECEPTION

Arrival of the Bride & Groom

For continuity, it would be appropriate to play the music used for your recessional. If you'd prefer something different, I would suggest something lively to put everyone in a dancing mood - *Crowley's Reel*, for example, by James Galway & The Chieftains. It's on their *In Ireland* recording.

Receiving line, Cocktail hour and Dinner music

The following is a list of suggested cuts that can be played by your DJ or musicians.

CD	Selection	Track #
Celtic Odyssey	Ramble To Cashel	1
Celtic Hymns	The King of Love	10
The Lark In The Clear Air (Galway)	Lark in the Clear Air	3
Film Cuts (Chieftains)	Air-You're The One	3
Eyna	Fairytale	8
Eyna	Epona	9
The Fairie Round	Planxty Burke	9
In Ireland (Galway/Chieftains)	Down by the Sally Gardens	4
In Ireland (ditto)	Maggie	12
Clannad In Concert	Neansaí Mhíle Grá	9
Voyager (Michael Oldfield)	Song of the Sun	1
Voyager (ditto)	Celtic Rain	2
Watermark (Eyna)	On Your Shore	3
Film Cuts (Chieftains)	Tristan & Isolde	13
Annam (Clannad)	Harry's Game	7
Crossing To Ireland (Clarke/Johnson)	The Slumbering Minstrel	18
Shadow of Time (Nightnoise)	The Rose of Tralee	11
Celtic Harp (Chieftains)	Madame Cole	5
Celtic Harp (ditto)	Planxty Bunting	4
Something of Time (Nightnoise)	Wiggy Wiggy	7

Cake Cutting

The Irish Wedding Song Andy Cooney, *A Collection of Irish Hits*

Special Dances

Aside from the newlywed's first dance, many couples are dispensing with the formalities of special dances for the father/daughter, mother/son and so on. But just in case you want to stay with tradition, you can purchase a recording from Rego Records called a *Wedding Song Collection* which features many old favorites performed by some of Ireland's most popular artists. And yes, it does include *Daddy's Little Girl!* You may also wish to consider honoring the counties from which your families are from and include selections with the name of the county or a place in the title. Some suggestions that immediately spring to mind are *The Mountains of Mourne, The Isle of Innisfree, Galway Bay, Home to Mayo* and *The Rose of Tralee.* You might also wish to consider one or more of the following:

Father/Daughter Dance

My Wild Irish Rose. It's been recorded by many artists including a great version by the Mills Brothers. You can also purchase it from Rego Records on a collection called *130 Irish Party Songs* which includes almost all of the old standards.

Mother/Son Dance

Never Be the Sun. Dolores Keane, *Celtic Tapestry.*
The Green Glens of Antrim. Carmel Quinn, *They Call It Ireland*
Danny Boy. James Galway & *The Chieftains In Ireland*

Parents' Dance

Love's Old Sweet Song. Jim McCann, *Grace*
Slíabh na mBán. Druidstone, *The Vow - An Irish Wedding Celebration*

Tossing the Bouquet/Garter

When Irish Eyes Are Smiling just might be perfect for these two events! Worth considering, even if it isn't authentically Irish, and available on literally hundreds of recordings.

Presenting the Groom

It was once traditional in Ireland for the groomsmen to place the new husband in a chair, lift him up (chair included) and parade him around the room. *O'Sullivan's March* from *The Best of The Chieftains* album has just the right tempo!

General Dancing

The great advantage with Irish music, both contemporary and traditional, is that you can vary the pace and the mood. From romantic ballads to hard rock, and everything in between, there's so much available that you probably won't have time to play everything you'd like. But have fun trying!

THE IRISH WEDDING SONG
Here they stand hand in hand.
They've exchanged wedding bands.
Today is the day they have sealed all their plans.
And all we who love them have gathered to to say,
God bless this couple who married today.

In good times and bad times, in sickness and health,
May they know that riches are not needed for wealth.
And help them face problems they'll meet on their way,
Oh God bless this couple who married today.

May they find peace of mind comes to all who are kind.
May the trials ahead become triumphs in time.
May any children be happy as they.
Oh God bless this family who started today.

As they go may they know a real love that will show.
And as life gets shorter may their feelings grow.
Wherever they travel, wherever they stay,
May God bless this couple* who married today.

* Substitute first names of the bride and groom in the last line of the song, e.g. May God bless 'Cáitlín and Owen who married today.'

II
RECIPES

Laughter is brighter where food is best.

In this section the recipes follow the order of their appearance in the book. Thus, all of the suggestions for the pre-wedding parties are first, then the reception, and finally, the post-wedding menus. After the recipes, in Information Section III, is a calendar of saints' feast-days and information about the foods traditionally served. Where possible, recipes are written to accommodate cooks all over the world.

PRE-WEDDING PARTIES

Aitin' The Gander Dinner
Darina Allen runs the world-renowned Ballymaloe Cookery School in County Cork. She has also written several cookbooks and this recipe is adapted from *The Festive Food of Ireland*.

Michaelmas Goose with Potato Apple Stuffing
Ingredients
1 goose, weighing about 10 lb. with giblets,
neck, heart and gizzard
1 small onion
1 carrot
Bouquet garni consisting of 1 sprig of thyme, 3 or 4 parsley stalks,
a small piece of celery
6 or 7 peppercorns
roux, if desired, for thickening
Stuffing
2 lbs. potatoes
1/2 stick butter
1 lb. onions, chopped
1 lb. Bramley, Granny Smith or other tart cooking
apples, peeled and chopped
1-1 1/2 tablespoons chopped parsley
1-1 1/2 tablespoons lemon balm
salt and freshly ground pepper

1. First make the stuffing. Boil the unpeeled potatoes in salted water until cooked; peel and mash.

2. Melt the butter and sweat the onions in a covered saucepan on a gentle heat for about 5 minutes.

3. Add the apples and cook until they break down into a fluff, then stir in the mashed potatoes and herbs. Season with salt and pepper. Allow to get quite cold before stuffing the goose.

4. Gut the goose and singe if necessary. Remove the wishbone for ease of carving. Put the goose into a saucepan with the giblets, onion, carrot, bouquet garni and peppercorns. Cover with cold water, bring to the boil and simmer for about 2 hours. (The wing tips may also be added to the stock if desired.)

5. Remove the bird from the stock and pat dry. Season the cavity with salt and pepper and fill with the cold stuffing. Sprinkle some sea salt over the breast and rub into the skin. Roast for 2 - 2 1/2 hours in a preheated 350°F oven. Pour off the excess fat three or four times during the cooking (and store this fat in your refrigerator as it keeps for months and is wonderful for roasting or sautéeing potatoes). To test whether the goose is cooked, prick the thigh at the thickest part. The juices that run out should be clear; if they are pink, the goose needs cooking a little longer. When cooked, remove the goose to your best large serving dish and put it into a low-heat oven while you make the gravy.

6. To make the gravy, pour or spoon off the remainder of the fat. Add about 2 1/2 cups of strained giblet stock to the roasting tin, bring to the boil and, using a small whisk, scrape the tin well to dissolve the meaty deposits. Taste for seasoning and if you wish,

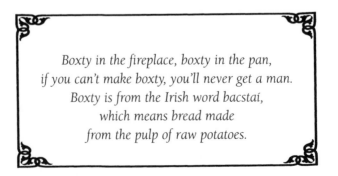

Boxty in the fireplace, boxty in the pan,
if you can't make boxty, you'll never get a man.
Boxty is from the Irish word bacstaí,
which means bread made
from the pulp of raw potatoes.

thicken with a little roux. If the gravy is weak, boil for a few minutes to concentrate the flavor; if too strong, add a little water or stock. Strain and serve.

7. Bring the goose to the table and carve. Serve apple sauce and gravy separately.

Makes eight to ten servings.
Note: A goose looks enormous but it has a large carcass. Allow at least 1 lb. uncooked weight per person.

Jane FitzGerald's Blue Ribbon Feis Soda Bread

I've known Jane for nearly 30 years and we've shared so much that we're more like sisters than best friends. She is incredibly accomplished in the kitchen and has won first and second prizes for her breads and cakes. This recipe won first place at the 1997 Cincinnati Feis.

Ingredients
3 1/2 cups all-purpose flour
1 1/2 to 2 tablespoons caraway seeds (optional)
1 teaspoon baking soda
1 teaspoon salt
1 1/2 cups buttermilk

Preheat oven to 425°F. Lightly grease, then flour baking sheet. In large bowl, mix flour, baking soda, salt and optional caraway seeds. Mix in buttermilk to form dough into ball. You may need to add a little more buttermilk. Turn out onto lightly floured surface and knead until dough holds together, about 1 minute. Shape dough into a six-inch round. Place on prepared baking sheet. Cut one-inch deep X across top of bread, reaching almost to edges. Bake until bread is golden brown and sounds hollow when tapped on bottom, about 40 minutes.Transfer bread to rack and cool. If not serving right away, wrap loaf in tea towel to prevent it from drying out too much. If not eaten in entirety, wrap well in foil or plastic wrap to keep as moist as possible.

Bunratty Apple Tart

From *Cooking With Irish Spirits* by Margaret Johnson.

Ingredients

4 medium Bramley, Granny Smith, or other tart
cooking apples, peeled, cored and sliced
1/4 cup sugar
2 tablespoons Bunratty Meade
1 cup flour
6 oz. butter
1 tablespoon sugar
1 egg yolk
2 tablespoons water

Preheat oven to 350°F. Arrange sliced apples on the bottom of a greased eight-inch pie plate. Sprinkle with the sugar and Bunratty Meade. Make a pastry crust by blending the remaining ingredients to form a soft dough. Turn onto a floured board, knead and roll to cover the pie plate. Crimp the edges. Bake for 45 to 50 minutes, or until the crust is nicely browned. Serve warm with vintage Irish cheddar cheese or whipped cream.Serves 8.

HEN PARTY

Therese O'Flaherty's Cucumber Sandwiches

My sister-in-law Therese can't turn up at a party unless she brings a plateful of these delicious open-face sandwiches. Deceptively simple to make, they're totally addictive.

Ingredients

1 large cucumber, sliced very thin
Pillsbury Pop'n Fresh Bread Dough or equivalent
(refrigerator section of grocery store)
low-fat cream cheese
dill weed
salt to taste

Place bread dough in cylinder shaped baking mold. Follow directions on back of bread package and bake. Once cooled, slice into thin rounds. Spread cream cheese on rounds and sprinkle with dill. Place thin cucumber slice on each round and lightly sprinkle with salt, if desired. Chill. Serve cold.

Drop Scones

This recipe is adapted from one I found on the The Irish Studies website which was created by Conrad Jay Bladey, a lecturer of Irish history, customs and folklore. If you have access to the world wide web, the site is filled with an amazing variety of Irish-related topics. Well worth browsing!

Ingredients

2 cups all-purpose flour

1 level teaspoon cream of tartar

1/2 teaspoon baking soda

pinch of salt

1 level tablespoon of brown sugar

1 level tablespoon golden syrup

(Lyle's Golden Syrup is available in specialty food shops)

1 egg

1 pint milk

In a bowl, sift together flour, sugar, cream of tartar, baking soda and salt. Beat in the syrup, egg and milk to form a fairly thick batter. Lightly grease and heat a griddle or heavy skillet. Drop in tablespoon full of the batter and cook over moderate heat until bubbles appear on the surface. Turn and cook on the other side. Remove and place in a tea towel until ready to serve. Serve with butter and a variety of jams or jellies. Makes 15 scones.

---

*In Ulster, when a man feigned
interest in a girl because she or her
people kept a good table,
he was labeled a belly bachelor.*

*In ancient Ireland,
badgers were considered a delicacy,
as were porpoise and seals.*

Strawberry Scones

This is also from Conrad Bladey's Irish Studies Pages:

Ingredients

1 cup strawberries
2 1/2 cups all-purpose flour
3 tablespoons sugar
2 teaspoons baking powder
1/4 teaspoon salt
6 tablespoons butter
2/3 cup milk

Preheat oven to 425°F.

Cut strawberries in 1/2 inch pieces and set aside. In large bowl, mix together flour, sugar, baking powder and salt. Add butter. With pastry blender or two knives, cut in butter until mixture resembles coarse crumbs. Stir in reserved strawberries and toss well to coat. Add milk all at once. With a fork, lightly toss until mixture holds together. With floured hands, gently form into a ball. Gently roll out dough on floured board until 1/2 inch thick. Cut dough into two and a half inch circles with floured biscuit cutter. Place on greased cookie sheet. Bake until golden, about 12 minutes. Serve warm with whipped cream. Makes 12 scones.

Profiteroles (cream puffs)

From *Cooking with Irish Spirits* by Margaret Johnson.

Ingredients

1/2 cup butter
1 1/4 cups water
3/4 cup flour
pinch of salt
4 eggs, beaten

Preheat oven to 400°F. Put the butter and water in a saucepan and melt over low heat. When butter has melted, bring mixture it to a full boil and add flour and salt immediately, beating mixture until it forms a thick paste. Remove from heat and set aside until just warm. Gradually add eggs, beating thoroughly after each addition. The paste should be smooth and glossy. Place spoonfuls of the the paste on a greased baking tray, leaving room between each spoonful to allow for expansion. Bake for 30 minutes, or until well risen and crisp. Remove and make a slit in each one to allow steam to escape. Cool on a wire rack.

Fill with whipped cream and top with Baileys Hot Chocolate Sauce.

Baileys Hot Chocolate Sauce

Ingredients
3 tablespoons cornstarch
2 cups water
2 tablespoons sugar
1 square semi-sweet chocolate
2 cups heavy cream
2 tablespoons Baileys Irish Cream

In a small saucepan, blend the cornstarch to a smooth paste with a little of the water. Add the remaining water. Stir over medium heat until boiling. Reduce the heat and simmer gently for two minutes, then add the sugar. Mix well. Break the chocolate into pieces and add to the sauce. Continue stirring over low heat until the chocolate has melted. Add the cream and Baileys. Heat gently, without boiling, for an additional two minutes.

Irish oysters, according to tradition, are thought to be an aphrodisiac and are particularly potent when accompanied by a pint of stout - even more risky, so they say in Ireland, than standing under the mistletoe!

Pork was such an important part of Ireland's agricultural wealth that the pig was often referred to by farmers as 'the gentleman who pays the rent.'

In ancient Ireland, meat and salmon were eaten with a flavoring of honey. Often, a dish of honey was put on the table and diners would use it as we use bottled sauces.

Irish Mist Cheesecake

This is from from *Cooking with Irish Spirits* by Margaret Johnson who got it from the Dun Aonghasa Restaurant, Kilronan, Aran Islands.

Ingredients
3/4 cup digestive biscuits, crumbled
1/4 cup butter
8 envelopes gelatin
1/2 cup warm water
1 1/4 lbs. cream cheese
1/2 cup Irish Mist Liqueur
5 large eggs separated
3/4 cup sugar
1 cup heavy cream, lightly whipped

Melt butter and mix with biscuit crumbs. Press into a nine-inch springform pan. Soak gelatin in cold water and strain when softened. Add to warm water to dissolve. Add Irish Mist Liqueur. In a large bowl, cream the cheese, add egg yolks and sugar. Beat until mixture is smooth. When thoroughly creamed, mix in gelatin. Fold in whipped cream. Whip egg white and fold into mixture. Turn into crust and chill for at least two hours.

Tea – for the talkin'

I can still hear my mother saying, "Now Bridget, be a good girl won't ye, and make a nice cup of tae for your poor old mother." I think she might have been around 45 years old at the time! At quite an early age, I was taught, as were the majority of Irish daughters not so long ago, how to make a perfect 'cupan tae.'

Ingredients
cold water
bulk Irish tea
whole milk or half and half
sugar

Fill a kettle with cold water fresh from the faucet. Bring to a boil and be ready to use right away. While you are bringing the water to a boil, have ready a teaspoon to measure out the tea, a strainer, teapot (earthenware is best), and a tea cozy or towel. Warm the teapot by pouring in some hot water from the faucet and then pouring it out. Bring the teapot to the stove and as soon as the water boils, fill the teapot. Put one heaping teaspoon of tea per cup into the teapot, plus one more 'for the pot'. Put lid on immediately and then cover the teapot with a cozy or towel. Keep in a warm place and let the tea steep for a five full minutes. In the meantime, prepare the cups. My mother always insisted that the milk go in before the tea. But she would never allow anyone to put in her sugar. That was 'stirring up trouble!' Pour plenty of milk or cream into the cup, place the strainer so it's resting on the cup, and pour in the tea. After tea, be sure to save the tea leaves, especially if you're a rose grower. They're a great food for plants that like acids and my mother's gorgeous garden was sure proof of that.

BRIDESMAIDS' LUNCHEON

King Sitric Brown Bread

This recipe is from *Classic Irish Recipes* by Georgina Campbell who got it from the King Sitric, a renowned seafood restaurant in County Dublin. According to Georgina, it is interesting to note that this recipe seems to have a direct line of descent from the old bastable oven, as it is cooked in a cast iron casserole with the lid on.

Ingredients

4 2/3 cups coarse whole wheat flour, preferably stone ground

1 cup all-purpose flour

1 rounded teaspoon baking soda

1 teaspoon salt

2 teaspoons sugar

2 1/2 cups buttermilk

2 tablespoons melted butter

Preheat oven to 425°F. Heat a 1 1/2-2 quart cast-iron casserole with a lid. Mix the flours, soda, salt and sugar in a large bowl; add the buttermilk and mix thoroughly to make a very wet mixture. Mix in the melted butter and turn into the hot casserole, then cover with the lid and bake in the oven for 1 hour, removing the lid for the last 10 minutes to allow the top to brown. Remove from the oven and turn the loaf onto a wire rack; wrap in a damp linen towel and leave to cool.

Makes 1 large loaf.

Cold Chicken in Tarragon Sauce

This is a very easy recipe to prepare and is especially appropriate for a summer luncheon. I like to use a good quality Chardonnay, especially while I'm making it!

Ingredients

3 to 4 lbs. whole chicken with giblets

salt and pepper

tarragon leaves (fresh is best, but dried will do)

1 onion cut into quarters

1 carrot cut into quarters

1 stick celery cut into quarters

1 bay leaf

1/4 cup butter

1/2 cup flour

6 oz. of dry white wine

2 teaspoons chopped parsley

juice of 1/2 lemon

3 to 4 tablespoons whipped cream

3 to 4 tablespoons mayonnaise

Garnish of tarragon sprigs and lemon rind

Chicken

Sprinkle the inside of the chicken with salt, pepper and tarragon leaves. Place the onion, carrot, and celery in a saucepan just big enough to accommodate the chicken. Put in the chicken, breast side up, and pour in enough water to cover it. Cover pan tightly and bring to a boil. Reduce heat and simmer for about an hour. Remove the pan from the heat and turn the chicken breast side down in the stock. Be careful not to break the skin. Put the lid back on the pan and allow to cool. When cool enough to handle, remove the chicken from the stock. Remove and discard the skin and slice all the meat from the bones. Refrigerate until ready to serve. Measure out 1 1/4 cups of stock for the sauce and refrigerate the rest.

Sauce

Melt the butter in a heavy saucepan. Stir in the flour and cook for a minute or two. Add the white wine. Gradually stir in the 1 1/4 cups of stock. Add tarragon, parsley and lemon juice and bring the sauce to a boil. Cook for an additional two minutes, stirring continuously. Remove from heat and allow to cool slightly. When cooled, gently fold in the whipped cream and then the mayonnaise. Toss chicken in about 3/4 of the sauce and arrange on a large, shallow serving platter. Spoon on the remainder of the sauce and garnish with tarragon sprigs and lemon rind before serving. Makes six to eight servings.

New Potatoes

According to Anthony Bluett, author of *Things Irish*, new potatoes should be placed in water that has already come to a boil, unlike regular potatoes which should be put in cold water which is then heated to boiling.

Ingredients
1 to 2 unpeeled red potatoes per person
1/4 to 1/2 lb butter, melted
salt & freshly ground pepper to taste
chopped scallions

Scrub potatoes and leave skins on. Bring water to the boil and add potatoes. Reduce heat and simmer gently until the potatoes are fork-tender. Drain and then toss with melted butter. Season with salt and pepper and toss with chopped scallions. Serve immediately.

Warm Spinach Salad

This is from *Cooking with Irish Spirits* by Margaret Johnson.

Ingredients
8 cups fresh spinach
1/2 lb. bacon
1/2 cup wine vinegar
2 tablespoons Worcestershire Sauce
4 tablespoons lemon juice
1/2 cup sugar
1 cup Bunratty Meade
Freshly ground black pepper

Wash spinach, dry thoroughly and place in salad bowl. Sauté the bacon until crisp, then drain on paper towels. Pour off bacon fat from pan except for four tablespoons. To the four tablespoons of bacon fat, add vinegar, Worcestershire, lemon juice, and sugar. Bring to a boil and cook for about three minutes. Pour over the spinach. Add Bunratty Meade to the pan and carefully flame. When flame dies out, pour it over the salad. Crumble the bacon over the salad, add ground pepper and toss thoroughly. Makes four to eight servings.

Apple Snow

This is from *Classic Irish Recipes* by Georgina Campbell.
Ingredients
1 1/2 lbs. Granny Smith, Bramley or other tart cooking apples
3 tablespoons water
2 pieces thinly peeled lemon rind (optional)
1/2 cup sugar
3 egg whites

Peel and core the apples, slice into a saucepan and add the water and lemon rind, if using. Cover and simmer gently until the apples 'fall' - about 15 minutes. Remove from the heat, remove the lemon rind and mix in the sugar. Make a purée by mixing in a blender, putting through a food mill or rubbing through a sieve. Set aside until cool. Whisk the egg whites until stiff, then carefully fold into the purée with a metal spoon. Put into glass serving dishes and chill. Serve with brown sugar and whipped cream or crumbled cookies. Makes six servings.

Carolans Chip Cookies

This is from *Cooking with Irish Spirits* by Margaret Johnson.
Ingredients
1/2 cup butter
3/4 cup light brown sugar
1 egg
1 cup flour
1/2 teaspoon baking soda
1/4 teaspoon salt
1/3 cup Carolans Irish Cream
3/4 teaspoon vanilla
3/4 cup semi-sweet chocolate morsels

Preheat oven to 375°F. Beat butter and sugar together until light and fluffy. Beat in egg. Sift flour with baking soda and salt. Add to butter mixture alternately with Carolans and vanilla. Stir in chocolate pieces. Drop batter by slightly rounded teaspoons onto a greased cookie sheet. Bake 10-12 minutes or until golden. Remove from pan and cool completely on wire racks. Makes three dozen.

STAG PARTY/BACHELORETTE PARTY

Ploughman's Lunch Sausage Rolls

I've been making these for years and always serve them with Colman's mustard (the dry, powdered variety). Mix the powder with malt vinegar and water to a spreadable consistency. Fair warning; it's hot enough to make your eyes water! A small dab goes a long way.

Ingredients
12 pork sausage links
1 package Pillsbury Crescent Rolls or best equivalent
(You'll find these in the refrigerator section at the supermarket and they are the kind of roll that comes in perforated triangles which are pulled apart and then normally rolled up into a crescent moon shape.)

Preheat oven to 425°F. Cook sausages according to directions on package. Set aside to cool. Unroll dough and instead of splitting into triangles, split so that two triangles remain attached. Cut with a sharp knife into three vertical slices. Wrap one sausage in pastry slice. Crimp edges to seal. Place on ungreased cookie sheet and bake until golden brown, about ten to 12 minutes. Cut each pastry into thirds and serve with toothpicks. Makes about 36 small sausage rolls.

Judith Flynn's Dublin Potato Salad

I became acquainted with Judith on the Internet while we were both researching our Irish roots. Since then, we've become dear friends. She has also been very generous in sharing memories of her honeymoon (See Chapter 8), as well as several recipes for the book.

Ingredients
2 tablespoons vinegar
1 teaspoon celery seed
1 teaspoon mustard seed
3 medium-large potatoes
2 teaspoons sugar
1 teaspoon salt
2 cups finely shredded uncooked cabbage
12-oz. corned beef, cooked, chilled, and cubed
1/4 cup finely chopped dill pickle
1/4 cup sliced green onion
1 cup real mayonnaise
1/4 cup milk

Combine vinegar, celery seed and mustard seed; set aside. Meanwhile, wash potatoes and cook them in their jackets in enough boiling water to cover until done (about 30 to 40 minutes). While potatoes are still warm, cube and then drizzle on vinegar mixture. Sprinkle with sugar and a half teaspoon of salt. Chill thoroughly. Before serving, add cabbage, corned beef, pickle, and green onion. Combine mayonnaise, milk and the second 1/2 teaspoon of salt. Pour over corned beef mixture and toss lightly. Makes 6 to 8 servings.

Irish Lamb Stew

Another recipe from Conrad Bladey's Irish Studies Pages.

Ingredients

1/2 lb thickly sliced bacon, diced

6 lbs. boneless lamb shoulder

1 teaspoon salt

1/2 teaspoon freshly ground pepper

1/2 cup all purpose flour

2 cloves garlic, peeled and finely chopped

1 large yellow onion, peeled and finely chopped

1/2 cup water

4 cups beef stock, canned or home-made

2 teaspoons sugar

4 cups carrots cut into 1-inch pieces

2 large yellow onions, peeled and sliced

3 lbs. potatoes peeled, quartered and cut into 1/2 inch pieces

1 teaspoon dried thyme, whole

1 bay leaf

1 cup dry white wine

Garnish: chopped parsley.

Sauté bacon in large frying pan. Reserve fat and bacon. Put lamb, salt, pepper and flour in large mixing bowl. Toss to coat meat evenly. Brown meat in frying pan with bacon fat. Put meat into a ten quart stove-top pot. Remove all but one 1/4 cup of fat in frying pan. Add the garlic and yellow onions and sauté till onion begins to color. Deglaze pan with 1/2 cup water and add the garlic-onion mixture to pot, along with bacon pieces, beef stock and sugar. Cover and simmer for 1 1/2 hours or till tender. Add remaining ingredients to pot and simmer for 20 minutes until vegetables are tender. Season to taste and top with parsley garnish. Makes enough for lots of lads!

Coffee and Walnut Gateau with Baileys Coffee Filling and Frosting

From *Cooking with Irish Spirits* by Margaret Johnson.

Ingredients
1/3 cup butter
3/4 cup sugar
2 eggs
1/2 teaspoon coffee extract
1 cup flour
2 teaspoons baking powder
1/2 teaspoon salt
1/4 cup milk
1/4 cup Baileys Irish Cream
1/2 cup walnuts, chopped

Preheat oven to 350°F. Cream the butter and sugar until light and fluffy. Add the eggs, one at a time, beating well after each addition. Stir in the coffee extract. Sift together flour, baking powder and salt. Add to the egg mixture, alternating with the milk and Baileys, until well blended. Fold in the walnuts. Grease and line two eight–inch cake pans with wax paper. Pour batter into pans and bake for 35-40 minutes, or until well risen and springy to the touch. Turn onto wire racks and cool. Remove wax paper and cool completely. Fill and frost with Baileys Coffee Frosting.

Baileys Coffee Frosting

Ingredients
1/2 cup unsalted butter
1 cup confectioners sugar, sifted
1/4 cup Baileys Irish Cream
1 teaspoon coffee extract
3 tablespoons milk
8-10 shelled walnut halves for decoration

Cream the butter and sugar. Mix well and stir in the Baileys and coffee extract. Add just enough milk to make the frosting smooth and easy to spread. Fill and frost the layers and sides. Decorate with walnut halves.

Irish Rarebit

Conrad Bladey has compiled an extensive collection of recipes on his Irish Studies Pages, including this one:

Ingredients
2 tablespoons butter
2 tablespoons flour
1 teaspoon honey
1/2 cup milk
1/2 cup Guinness Stout
1 cup sharp cheddar cheese, grated
salt and pepper to taste
toast made from thick slices of bakery bread

Melt the butter in a heavy pan and stir in the flour to make a roux. Cook over low heat for another minute, but don't let it brown. Remove pan from heat and gradually beat the milk into the roux. Return to heat and stir constantly until the mixture thickens. Stir in mustard and honey and then the Guinness. Cook sauce fairly rapidly for two to three minutes then add grated cheese and stir over very low heat only until the cheese has melted. Spread thickly on four thick slices of toast and brown under the grill. Makes four servings.

Traditional Irish Stew Made With Guinness Stout

From *Cooking with Irish Spirits* by Margaret Johnson, who got it from Gallagher's Boxty House in Dublin. Not all Irish stews are made with lamb or mutton as this delicious recipe demonstrates.

Ingredients
1/2 cup unsalted butter
3 lbs beef, cut into cubes
3 onions, chopped
2 cloves garlic, chopped
1 cup beef stock
2 tablespoons flour
1 tablespoon brown sugar
1 1/2 cups Guinness Stout
1 tablespoon wine vinegar
2 bay leaves

Preheat oven to 350°F. On top of the stove, melt butter in a heavy, oven-proof casserole. Brown the beef a little at a time, then add the garlic and onions and brown gently. Add stock and bring to a boil. Stir in the flour and brown sugar. Add Guinness, vinegar and bay leaves. Cook in a moderate oven for about two hours or until the beef reaches a desired tenderness. Serve with boiled potatoes or white rice. Makes four to six servings.

Colcannon

Even for the most inexperienced cook, this is a very easy dish to prepare.

Ingredients
1/2 cup finely chopped leek or scallions
1/4 cup butter
1/4 cup half and half milk
1lb. cooked potatoes, well mashed
1 1/2 cups cooked cabbage

Melt butter, add onion and gently fry until soft. Add the milk and the well mashed potatoes and stir until heated through. Finely chop the cabbage and beat it into the potato mixture over low heat or until the mixture is pale green and fluffy.

Dublin Coddle

The savior of many a Dubliner who'd spent a little too much time 'on the jar,' this dish was traditionally eaten when the men got home from the pub on a Saturday night. I've heard of many variations, most with potatoes, one without, another with tomatoes, yet another that calls for quail's eggs! I finally decided that simplest is best, so based on classic ingredients, I came up with the following recipe which serves four.

Ingredients
1/2 lb. thick bacon slices
1 lb. pork sausages
1 1/2 lbs. potatoes
1 lb. onions
salt and pepper to taste

Boil a kettle of water. Put the bacon and sausages in a saucepan with enough boiling water to cover. Bring back to the boil, then reduce heat and simmer for five minutes. Remove the bacon and sausages and carefully pour off the liquid from the saucepan into a bowl. Set aside. Peel and slice the potatoes and onions and place them with the bacon and sausages into a heavy saucepan or greased oven-proof casserole. Cover with the reserved liquid, season with salt and pepper and cover with a tight-fitting lid. Simmer on top of the stove or in a 350°F oven for about one hour.

REHEARSAL DINNER

AN IRISH COUNTRY DINNER

Boiled Ham & Cabbage With Parsley Sauce

In addition to a roast goose or duck, Christmas dinner at our house always included 'a bit of boiled ham' prepared by my father. The following recipe is an adaptation of how he used to fix it. The parsley sauce is a classic in Irish cooking, but my father preferred his ham and cabbage without any embellishments. Either way, this is a delicious dish at any time of year.

Ingredients
3 to 4 lbs. of uncooked ham
2 lbs. cabbage
1/2 medium onion
1/2 cup brown sugar
Cloves for studding the ham

Place ham in a large pot and cover with cold water. Bring to a boil, skim off fat, and simmer for 20 minutes per pound and then 20 minutes more. Meanwhile, cut cabbage into quarters and place in a large saucepan with the cut onion. When the ham is finished cooking, take three to four ladles of the stock and spoon it over the cabbage. Cover tightly and cook cabbage for about 20 minutes. While cabbage is cooking, remove skin from the ham and cut a lattice design on the fatty surface of the meat. Coat with brown sugar and stud with cloves. Brown in the oven. When cabbage is cooked, drain and remove onion.

Parsley Sauce

Ingredients
1 1/4 cups stock (from pan in which cabbage was cooked)
1/4 cup butter
3 tablespoons flour
1 1/4 cups milk
1/2 cup chopped parsley (fresh is best but dried will do)
Melt butter in a saucepan, stir in the flour until nice and smooth. Cook over low heat for a minute or two, being careful not to brown.

Gradually add the stock and then the milk. Bring to a boil, stirring constantly and cook for a few minutes until thickened. Add the chopped parsley. Season to taste. Serve with the ham, cabbage, and potatoes boiled in their jackets.

King Sitric Bread (see earlier recipe)

Irish Apple Cake

I found this recipe in *The Festive Food of Ireland* by Darina Allen.

Ingredients
2 cups white flour
1/4 teaspoon baking powder
1 stick butter
generous 1/2 cup castor sugar
1 egg beaten
1/4 to 1/2 cup milk
2-3 Bramley, Granny Smith, or other green cooking apples, peeled, cored and chopped
2-3 cloves (optional)
1 egg beaten with a pinch of salt, to glaze

1. Sieve the flour and baking powder into a bowl and rub in the butter. Add about two thirds of the sugar, the egg, and enough milk to form a soft dough.
2. Divide in two. Put one half onto a greased oven-proof plate and pat out with floured fingers to cover the plate.
3. Arrange the chopped apples and the cloves on the dough and sprinkle with the rest of the sugar, depending on the sweetness of the apples.
4. Roll out the remaining dough and cover the top. This is easier said than done as the dough is like a scone dough and is very soft. Press the sides together, cut a slit through the lid, brush with egg wash and bake for about 40 minutes in a 350°F oven.
5. Dredge with castor sugar and serve with soft brown sugar and softly whipped cream.

Makes six servings.

REMINISCENT OF THE BUNRATTY BANQUET

Leek & Potato Soup

This is a recipe I found by Georgina Campbell that appeared in The Romance of Ireland, a special collector's edition of *Bon Appetit* magazine.

Ingredients
3 tablespoons butter
3 large leeks (white and pale green parts only), halved
lengthwise, thinly sliced (about 4 1/2 cups)
2 large russet potatoes (about 18 ounces total), peeled, diced
4 1/2 cups (or more) chicken stock or canned low-salt broth
2 tablespoons chopped fresh chives

Melt butter in heavy large saucepan over medium heat. Add leeks; stir to coat with butter. Cover saucepan; cook until leeks are tender, stirring often, about ten minutes. Add potatoes. Cover and cook until potatoes begin to soften but do not brown, stirring often, about ten minutes. Add 4 1/2 cups stock. Bring to boil. Reduce heat, cover and simmer until vegetables are very tender, about 30 minutes. Purée soup in batches in processor until smooth. Return to saucepan. Thin with additional stock if soup is too thick. Season with salt and pepper. Ladle into bowls and garnish with chives. Makes four servings.

Note: Can be prepared one day ahead. Cover and refrigerate. When ready to serve, place in saucepan, cover, and bring slowly to a gentle simmer until heated through.

Heather and Honey Spareribs

This is from *Cooking with Irish Spirits* by Margaret Johnson.

Ingredients
1/2 cup soy sauce
1/4 cup tomato catsup
1/2 cup Bunratty Meade
2 cloves garlic or shallots, finely chopped
4 lbs. spare ribs
2 onions, thinly sliced
1/2 cup water
1 tablespoon honey

Preheat oven to 350°F. Mix together a marinade of soy sauce, catsup, Bunratty Meade, garlic (or shallots). Set aside. Arrange ribs in a flat roasting pan and cover with onions and water. Cover with foil and bake for one hour. Drain and place in marinade for four to five hours. Reserve two tablespoons of marinade for basting. Mix together reserved marinade and honey. Arrange marinated ribs in a flat roasting pan, cover with the honey and reserved marinade sauce and bake for another 30 to 35 minutes. Increase heat to 450°F for the last five minutes. Makes six to eight servings.

St. Brigid's Oaten Bread

Another recipe from Conrad Bladey's Irish Studies Pages.

Ingredients

1 cup flour

1 tablespoon sugar

3/4 teaspoon baking powder

1/4 teaspoon baking soda

1/4 teaspoon salt

3 tablespoons butter cut into small pieces

3/4 cup uncooked oatmeal flakes

1 egg

1/2 cup buttermilk

Preheat oven to 425°F. Grease baking sheet. Combine flour, sugar, baking powder, baking soda, and salt in bowl and mix. Add butter bits and cut in with knife until mixture is crumbly. Add oats and toss to combine. In another bowl, beat egg with buttermilk. Make a well in the dry ingredients. Pour in the egg mixture and mix with fork until crumbs hold together. Make dough into a ball and transfer to floured surface. Knead 20 to 25 times. Add flour if sticky. Pat dough into an eight-inch round and place on greased baking sheet. Score a deep cross in the bread but do not cut all the way through. Bake 15 to 20 minutes until brown.

Carolans Irish Blondies

This is from *Cooking with Irish Spirits* by Margaret Johnson.

Ingredients
1 cup sugar
1/4 cup butter, softened
1 egg
3/4 cup flour
1/4 cup Carolans Irish Cream
1/3 cup walnuts, chopped

Preheat oven to 350°F. Grease an eight-inch square baking pan. In bowl, beat sugar, butter, and egg together until light and fluffy. Stir in flour alternating with Carolans. Fold in nuts. Spread mixture into prepared pan. Bake 30 minutes until golden and firm on top. Cool on a wire rack. Cut into 16 squares. The flavor gets even better if kept overnight in a cool place.

ELEGANT IRISH FARE

Angels on Horseback

This is from *Classic Irish Recipes* by Georgina Campbell.

Ingredients
24 oysters in their shells
24 small slices of smoked bacon
fresh lemon juice
freshly ground black pepper

Use a blunt-ended oyster knife to shuck the oysters. Insert the end of the knife between the shells near the hinge and work it until you cut through the mussel that holds the shells together. Catch the oyster liquid in a bowl and discard the shells. Put the oysters into a pan with the strained liquid, bring to the boil over gentle heat, simmer very gently for two minutes, then drain. Trim the slices of bacon and stretch them by pressing with the back of a knifeblade. Sprinkle the oysters with a little lemon juice and freshly ground black pepper, then roll each one up in a bacon slice and thread onto fine skewers. Cook under a hot broiler until the bacon is crisp and sizzling, turning half way through so both sides are cooked. Push off the skewers and serve hot on cocktail sticks. Makes four to six servings.

Smoked Salmon Bisque

There are probably as many recipes for salmon as there are fish jumping out of the weir in Galway City, and the aroma of salmon smoking throughout the countryside in Connemara makes you want to stop at the nearest restaurant. Today, sides of oak-smoked salmon are readily available and not a bit need go to waste! When separating the flesh from the skin, save both the skin and the trimmings and use them to make this delicious soup.

Ingredients
skin and trimmings from a side of oak-smoked salmon
1 onion
1/2 dozen cloves
1 carrot
1 1/2 sticks of celery
bay leaf
1 teaspoon salt
several peppercorns
1/4 cup butter
1/2 cup flour
1 tablespoon tomato paste
8 oz. dry white wine
4 tablespoons heavy cream
1 tablespoon fresh parsley

Place skin and trimmings in a saucepan. Cut the carrot and celery into large pieces and stud the onion with cloves. Add vegetables to the pan. Cover the contents with cold water and add bay leaf, salt, and peppercorns. Cover pan, bring to the boil, and then simmer for about 30 minutes. Remove bay leaf. Remove the onion, take out the cloves and return onion to pan. With a slotted spoon, remove the fish and scrape off any flesh that remains. Return this to the pan. Carefully strain half the liquid into a bowl. In another large pan, melt the butter, and stir in the flour until it's smooth. Stir in tomato paste and gradually add strained stock, stirring constantly until it thickens. Add the white wine. Put the rest of the stock containing the fish and vegetables into the blender and run on the liquify setting for about 30 seconds. Add this to the soup. Test for seasoning. Place a spoonful of cream garnished with a little chopped parsley on top of each bowl before serving. Makes six to eight servings.

Mushroom Salad with Meade

This is from *Cooking with Irish Spirits* by Margaret Johnson.

Ingredients
2 tablespoons lemon juice
3 tablespoons Bunratty Meade
8 oz. fresh mushrooms, sliced very thin
4 stalks celery, sliced very thin
2 cups shredded Bibb and Boston lettuce
finely chopped parsley
freshly ground black pepper
lemon slices for garnish

Combine lemon juice and Bunratty Meade in a jar and shake well. Put mushrooms and celery in a shallow dish and pour on dressing. Refrigerate for several hours. Arrange lettuce on salad plates and spoon marinated mushrooms over. Sprinkle with chopped parsley and ground black pepper. Garnish with lemon slices. Makes four servings.

Traditional White Soda Bread

This recipe was given to me by my dear friend, Judith Flynn, who got it from a dear friend of hers, Mrs. Lenihan.

Ingredients
4 1/2 cups flour
1 cup sugar
1 teaspoon salt
1 teaspoon baking soda
1 teaspoon baking powder
3 teaspoons caraway seeds
1/4 lb. butter
1 large egg
1 3/4 cups buttermilk

Preheat oven to 375°F. Cut butter into all dry ingredients with a pastry blender. Add egg and buttermilk; stir well. Flour hands and form dough into a ball. Turn onto floured board and knead for a minute or so. Dough will be sticky. Grease a ten-inch cast iron skillet with a spray such as Bakers Joy or equivalent and turn dough into it. Make a deep cross on top. Bake at 375°F for 35 minutes and then reduce temperature to 350°F and bake an additional 35 minutes. Remove from pan and rub with butter.

Irish Whiskey Trifle

This is from *Cooking with Irish Spirits* by Margaret Johnson.

Ingredients
1 sponge cake
1 1/2 cups fresh or frozen raspberries (defrosted)
1/2 jar raspberry preserves
1/2 cup Jameson Irish Whiskey
1 cup custard sauce
whipped cream
raspberries for garnish

Split sponge cake into two layers. Spread slices with raspberry preserves and put back together. Cut layers into small bite-size cubes and place in a clear glass bowl. Add raspberries and sprinkle with Jameson. Pour custard sauce over cake and chill. Before serving, decorate with whipped cream and raspberries.

Custard Sauce

Ingredients
3 eggs or 6 yolks
1/4 cup granulated sugar
1/8 teaspoon salt
2 cups whole milk that has been brought to a boil
Jameson Irish Whiskey to taste

Beat eggs or yolks together until evenly blended. Add remaining ingredients and cook over very low heat or in a double boiler over hot, but not boiling water until the custard coats a spoon, about 6 to 8 minutes. Flavor with Jameson to taste and chill. Makes 2 1/2 cups.

RECEPTION

SOUPS AND STARTERS (APPETIZERS)

Leek & Potato Soup (see earlier recipe)
Angels on Horseback (see earlier recipe)

Malted Whiskey Liver Paté
This is from *Cooking with Irish Spirits* by Margaret Johnson.
Ingredients
1/2 cup butter
1 onion, finely chopped
1 garlic clove, peeled and crushed
1 1/2 chicken livers, well trimmed
salt and freshly ground pepper
1 tablespoon heavy cream
2 tablespoons tomato paste
1/4 cup Tyrconnell Irish Whiskey
chopped parsley

Sauté onions and garlic in melted butter without browning until soft and transparent. Add chicken livers and cook for five to seven minutes. Centers should still be pink. Remove from heat and add remaining ingredients. Put in blender and process until smooth. Turn into a small mold or bowl. Sprinkle with chopped parsley. Serve with water biscuits, toast, or crackers. Makes eight to ten servings.

Dublin Bay Prawn Cocktail
In Ireland, shrimp are called prawns and the country is particularly fortunate as large, succulent prawns are plentiful. While I've seen several different recipes for this appetizer, the one that follows is my own adaptation.
Ingredients
4-5 lbs. cooked, deveined medium or large shrimp
1 head of top-quality lettuce, chopped and shredded
8 tablespoons real mayonnaise
8 tablespoons whipped cream

1/2 teaspoon Worcestershire Sauce
2 teaspoons grated fresh horseradish
salt and pepper to taste
chopped parsley

   Chill shrimp and heap on shredded lettuce bed in a large salad bowl. Make sauce by thoroughly mixing all remaining ingredients together. Serve sauce in bowl on side.
Note: If served individually, use stemmed glasses and pile shrimps on lettuce beds. Serve sauce poured over or on the side. Serves about 20.

BREADS (select from earlier recipes)

SALADS AND VEGETABLES

Mushroom Salad with Meade (see earlier recipe)
Colcannon (see earlier recipe)
Cabbage with Parsley Sauce (see earlier recipe)

Spinach Salad with Mustard Meade Vinaigrette
This is from *Cooking with Irish Spirits* by Margaret Johnson.
Ingredients
1/3 cup oil
1 tablespoon cider vinegar
3 tablespoons Bunratty Meade
2 tablespoons Dijon Mustard
2 tablespoons toasted sesame seeds
1 clove garlic or shallot, peeled and minced
1/2 teaspoon freshly ground black pepper
4 cups young, fresh spinach leaves
toasted croutons

   Place first seven ingredients in a jar and shake until thoroughly blended. Wash spinach. Dry thoroughly on paper towels. Place in salad bowl, pour on dressing and toss gently. Sprinkle with croutons. Makes two to four servings.

ENTRÉES

Chicken Cashel Blue

Yet another great recipe from *Cooking with Irish Spirits* by Margaret Johnson.

Ingredients

4 boneless chicken breasts

1/2 cup Cashel Blue cheese

flour seasoned with garlic salt for dredging chicken

1 egg plus 1 tablespoon milk, beaten together

1/2 cup fresh breadcrumbs

2 tablespoons cooking oil

2 tablespoons olive oil

3 shallots chopped

3/4 cup fresh mushrooms, sliced

2 tablespoons Jameson Irish Whiskey

1/4 cup half and half cream (which is called

'single' cream in Ireland)

fresh watercress

Preheat oven to 350°F. Make an incision in each breast to form a pocket. Roll Cashel Blue cheese into four cylindrical shapes and stuff each breast pocket. Dredge chicken in seasoned flour, dip in egg mixture and coat with fresh breadcrumbs. Heat cooking oil in pan and sauté chicken over medium heat until lightly browned, turning to cook evenly, about ten minutes. Transfer chicken to overproof baking dish and bake in preheated oven for additional 20 minutes. While chicken is baking, heat olive oil in same pan in which chicken was cooked and sauté chopped shallots. Add mushrooms and whiskey and cook slightly. Remove from the heat, add the cream and blend. Transfer sauce to a serving dish, place the chicken breasts into the sauce and garnish with fresh parsley. Makes four servings.

Limerick Ham

Another traditional Irish dish that can be prepared in a number of different ways. This recipe is from Conrad Bladey's Irish Studies Pages.

Ingredients
One ham, cured and cooked*
1/4 cup juniper berries (if dried, soak until soft)
1 1/2 cups Dijon country-style mustard
1 cup gin
1 cup brown sugar

Preheat oven to 350°F. Score ham to a half-inch depth on all sides. Rub juniper berries into the cuts all over. Mix the gin, brown sugar and mustard. Cover the ham with foil and bake until heated through (about ten minutes per pound). Remove foil and continue baking until skin is crisp. From time to time, baste with liquid from bottom of pan.
*In Ireland, they boil the ham first and and then bake it. Elsewhere, fully cooked water-cured hams are readily available and are suitable for this recipe.

Spiced Beef

Perfect for a buffet, because this dish is actually better served cold and sliced very thin. The recipe is from Conrad Bladey's Irish Studies Pages and I must confess, I haven't tested it; so a word of caution about the two pints of Guinness – it might be one for the pot and one for the cook!

Ingredients
20 cloves
2 teaspoons ground allspice or cinnamon
6 shallots
2 teaspoons. saltpeter*
1 lb Kosher salt
1 teaspoon. freshly ground black pepper
3 teaspoons ground mace
7 to 8 lb sirloin tip or eye of round roast
2 or 3 bay leaves
pinch of ground nutmeg
two pints of Guinness Stout

Grind all dry ingredients and mix together. Finely chop shallots and add to dry ingredients. Rinse beef and place in a plastic, glass or earthenware container. Avoid using a metal dish. Measure out approximately one seventh of spice/salt mixture and rub it all over the meat. Cover meat and refrigerate. Each day, for the next six days, rub another seventh of the spice/salt mixture into the meat and turn it over. Leave the juices being drawn from the meat in the bowl. After seven days, tie a string around the beef and put it into a large pot along with any juices. Cover with water, bring to a boil, reduce heat and simmer slowly for several hours until the beef is fork-tender. Be careful not to overdo it – a fork should just be able to lift up a strand of meat. Remove beef from the pan, pour off the water and replace with clean water to cover. Bring to boil and simmer for 30 minutes, then add the two pints of Guinness and simmer for another ten to 20 minutes. Serve hot or cold. If serving cold, place the beef on a platter to cool and then refrigerate with a weighted plate on top of it. Makes eight servings.

SIZE	6"/15cm	9"/23cm	12"/30cm
Butter	6oz/175g/1 1/2 sticks	12oz/350g/3 sticks	1 1/2lb/700g/6 sticks
Soft brown sugar	6oz/175g/2/3 cup	12oz/350g/1 1/2 cups	1 1/2lb/700g/2 1/2 cups
Eggs	3	6	12
Plain flour (all-purpose)	8oz/225g/2 cups	1lb/450g/4 cups	2lbs/900g/8 cups
Mixed spice	1/4 tsp/1.25ml	1/2 tsp/2.5ml	1 tsp/5ml
Salt	pinch	1/4 tsp	1/2tsp
Sultanas	8oz/225g/1 1/4 cups	1lb/450g/2 1/2 cups	2lbs/900g/5 cups
Currants	4oz/100g/3/4 cup	1/2lb/225g/1 1/2 cups	1lb/450g/3 cups
Raisins	6oz/175g/1 cup	12oz/350g/2 cups	1 1/2lb/700g/4 cups
Cut mixed peel	3oz/75g/1/2 cup	6oz/175g/1 cup	12oz/350g/2 cups
Glacé cherries	3oz/75g/2/3 cup	6oz/175g/1 1/2 cup	12oz/350g/3 cups
Chopped prunes	2oz/50g/1/4 cup	4 oz/100g/1/2 cup	8oz/225g/1 cup
Chopped dates	2oz/55oz/1/2 cup	4oz/100g/1 cup	8oz/225g/ 1 3/4 cups
Golden syrup (Karo)	1tbsp/15ml	2tbsp/30ml/	4tbsp/60ml
Almonds (Chopped)	2oz/50g/1/3 cup	4oz/100/2/3 cup	8oz/225g/1 1/2

*Saltpeter is available in most pharmacies.

DESSERT

Caragh Lodge Wedding Cake

This recipe is from Georgina Campbell's The Best of Irish Breads & Baking. It is a traditional family recipe given to Georgina by Mary Gaunt of County Kerry. Mary's mother, Moira Curtin, passed it on to her. The recipe calls for square cake pans. If you would prefer a round cake, use pans a size larger.(7"/10"/13"). Because you will be so busy with other details, I would suggest that you give the recipe to a professional baker, and keep in mind that this cake must sit for a month to six weeks to bring out the flavors. Also, please note that I have observed what appear to be discrepancies in the quantities and in the metric-to-ounces conversions. I defer to the judgement of a professional baker to interpret this table of measures.

Ingredients according to tin size (square).
Brandy or whiskey as required

1. Measure out the butter and sugar. Sift the flour with mixed spice and salt. Along with the eggs, leave in a warm atmosphere for seven to eight hours, or overnight. Measure out all the fruits. Add just enough brandy or other alcohol to barely cover and leave to soak overnight.

2. Grease the tins and line base and sides with a double layer of buttered greaseproof/waxed paper, which should extend at least 2"/5cm above the rim of the tins. Tie a thick band of folded brown paper or newspaper around the outside of the tins to protect the cakes during the long cooking.

3. Cream butter and sugar very well. Add eggs, one at a time, and beat well between additions. Add a little flour with the eggs if the mixture is inclined to curdle. Add the fruit mixture, syrup, and almonds. Mix well, then add the flour. The mixture should drop slowly from a wooden spoon.

4. Turn into the prepared tin(s) and smooth the top with the back of a spoon. Bake in the center of a very cool oven, preheated to 300°F for 1/2 hour. Reduce temperature to 275°F.

   Accurate cooking times are impossible to give, as ovens vary considerably. As a rough guide, allow about three to three and a half hours for the smallest cake, four to four and a half hours for the medium and as much as twice that for the largest cake. The important thing is to keep an eye on the cakes, checking at regular intervals: after one hour for the small cake, and after two to three hours for the larger ones. Be prepared to protect from over-browning by laying paper or foil loosely over top.

When cooked, the cakes shrink slightly from the sides of the tin and the top should feel firm when pressed lightly with the fingers. A clean, warmed skewer thrust into the center of the cake should come out clean, with no uncooked mixture clinging to it. If uncertain whether the cake is cooked through (particularly in the case of the largest one), a test plug can be removed from the centre of the cake.

Unless you have a large fan oven, which has the benefit of more even heat so the two smaller cakes could probably be cooked together, it is normally better to bake the cakes separately. Fan ovens cook more quickly than conventional ones but are inclined to dry cakes out. Consult your manufacturer's manual for guidance on temperature and timing.

Whatever oven is used, keep a close eye on progress and use your common sense. Cool the cooked cakes in the tins, then remove the papers and turn upside down onto a board. Make a lot of small holes all over the base with a skewer and pour in some extra brandy - about two to three fl oz/60ml/1/4 cup for the small cake; seven fl oz/200ml/2/3 cup for the medium one; and nine fl oz/250ml/1 1/4 cups for the large one. When the brandy has been throughly absorbed, wrap the cold cakes in a double layer ofgreaseproof/waxed paper, then a layer of foil. Seal and store in a cool place for at least a month, until you are ready to finish the cake about a fortnight* before the wedding.

Hints:

- For a 3-tier wedding cake, a 3"/7.5 cm difference between tiers looks 'well-balanced', as given above. For a 4-tier cake, 2"/5 cm difference is enough. Cake boards need to be 1 1/2"-2"/3.5 - 5 cm bigger than the cake.
- If you have a favorite Christmas cake recipe and want to make a simple 2-tier cake, it can be adapted quite easily. Use the

quantities given for an 8"/20 cm square or 9"/23 cm round cake for the base and halve them to make a square 6"/15 cm or round 7"/18 cm for the top layer period.

* A fortnight is equal to two weeks.

Author's note: Traditionally, an Irish wedding cake has almond paste spread on each layer and is then iced with water icing and royal icing.

Irish Coffee

This is the original recipe created in 1942 by Joe Sheridan at Foynes Airbase in Co. Limerick.

Ingredients:

1 jigger Irish whiskey

coffee

heavy cream

brown sugar

Fill glass with hot water to preheat, then empty. Pour piping hot coffee into the warmed glass until it is about 3/4 full. Add one table-spoon of brown sugar and stir until completely dissolved. Blend in Irish whiskey. Top with a collar of slightly whipped heavy cream by pouring gently over a spoon.

POST-WEDDING PARTIES

Bridget's Irish Breakfast

Ingredients
1 lb. Irish bacon
1 lb. Irish pork sausages
2 to 4 tomatoes
1/2 lb. white pudding
1/2 lb. black pudding
1 dozen eggs
1 lb. mushrooms
soda bread, Irish brown bread, or toasted white bread
marmalade

Depending on how many guests you're having, enlist the aid of someone to set the table, fix the toast, and brew the coffee and tea. Meanwhile, follow the cooking instructions that come with the imported Irish bacon, sausages, white pudding and black pudding. When the meats are cooked, put them on an oven-proof serving platter and place in a 300°F oven to keep warm. Sauté the mushrooms and tomatoes and place them on the meat platter. Eggs are the last to be cooked and we usually make it easy on ourselves by fixing them sunny side up for everyone.

Fadge or Potato Bread

This recipe is adapted from *The Festive Food Of Ireland* by Darina Allen.

Ingredients
2 lbs. unpeeled white potatoes
1 egg, beaten
1/4-1/2 stick butter
2 tablespoons/3 tablespoons flour
1-1 1/2 tablespoons chopped parsley, chives, and lemon thyme,
mixed (optional)
creamy milk
salt & freshly ground pepper
seasoned flour
bacon fat or butter for frying

1. Boil the potatoes in their jackets, pull off the skins and mash immediately.

2. Add the egg, butter, flour, and herbs (if using) and mix well. Season with plenty of salt and pepper, adding a few drops of creamy milk if mixture is too stiff.

3. Shape into a one inch-thick round and then cut into eight pieces. Dip in seasoned flour.

4. Bake on a griddle over an open fire or fry in bacon fat or melted butter on a gentle heat. Cook the fadge until crusty and golden on one side, then flip over and cook on the other side. (About four to five minutes on each side).

5. Serve with an Ulster Fry or on its own with a blob of butter melting on top.

Note: When you include fadge in a traditional Irish breakfast, the meal is called an Ulster Fry.

Boxty Pancakes

This is adapted from *The Festive Food of Ireland* by Darina Allen.

Ingredients

8 oz freshly cooked potatoes

8 oz peeled raw potatoes

2 cups white flour

1/4 teaspoon baking soda

1 to 1 1/2 cups buttermilk

pinch of salt (optional)

butter for frying

1. Peel the cooked potatoes while still hot and mash in a bowl.

2. Grate the raw potatoes and add to the mashed with the sieved flour and soda. Add salt if desired.

3. Mix well and add enough buttermilk to make a stiff batter.

4. Heat a frying-pan, grease with butter and cook large or small pancakes in the usual way.

5. Eat the pancakes straight from the pan with butter, crispy strips of bacon, or pure Irish honey.

Bacon and Egg Pie

This recipe is adapted from Conrad Bladey's Irish Studies Pages.

Ingredients

2 cups all-purpose flour

1 level teaspoon salt

1/3 cup lard

3 to 4 tablespoons cold water

1 lb. Irish bacon

6 eggs

Preheat oven to 400°F. Sift flour and salt into a bowl. With pastry blender, cut lard into flour. Gradually add the water, mixing it in with a knife until the mixture forms a ball and leaves the bowl clean. Lightly shape on a floured board and cut into two pieces. Grease a ten-inch pie plate, roll out half the pastry and line the pie plate. Place the bacon like the spokes of a wheel and break an egg into each space. Roll out the other half of the pastry and carefully cover the filling. Crimp the edges all around and lightly mark the segments with a knife so that each person gets a piece of bacon and an egg. Brush the top with milk. Bake for 40 to 45 minutes. Makes six servings.

III

CALENDAR OF SAINTS' FEAST DAYS, HOLIDAYS AND OTHER IMPORTANT OCCASIONS IN THE IRISH YEAR

In the old days, the season for marrying was between Christmas and Shrove Tuesday. It used to be forbidden to marry during Lent but New Year's Day, Shrove Tuesday and St Patrick's day were thought to be the luckiest days to tie the knot. The following calendar marks special occasions in Ireland and the foods that are traditionally served. Should your wedding day coincide with one of these dates, it might be wise to at least acknowledge the importance of the day by serving a sample of the traditional dish. Of course, if you're not superstitious, don't even give these suggestions a second thought!

Even though I could not find a traditional food for all of the Saints' feast days listed, should your wedding day fall on one of them, you might wish to have a prayer said to that Saint during your ceremony, or perhaps during the blessing of the meal at your reception. An asterisk indicates that a dish is included in the recipe section.

St. Mainchin	January 3
Twelfth Day	January 6

Nollaig na mBan, or Women's Christmas
High tea with all the trimmings enjoyed just by the women of the household or community. On January 7, the decorations were taken down, and in the old days, some of the holly and greenery was kept aside to heat the pancake griddle on Shrove Tuesday.

St. Ita	January 15
St. Aidan	January 31
St. Brigid	February 1

Boxty Pancakes * *eaten with freshly churned butter*

St. Brigid is the patron saint of cattle and dairy work and her cows are said to have produced more milk and better milk than any other herd. She is also known for performing a miracle when mead could not be found for the King of Leinster. According to the story, she blessed an empty vessel which miraculously became filled with mead. Afterwards, the fame of the brew made by Irish monks spread throughout medieval Ireland.

St. Mel	February 7
St. Fintan	February 17
St. Kieran	March 5
St. Senan	March 8
St. Patrick	March 17

Corned Beef and Cabbage

According to Irish friends, it's rarely eaten in Ireland, but it's still a sentimental favorite with the Irish diaspora. Originally, it was the traditional Easter Sunday dinner. The beef killed before the winter would have been salted and could now be eaten after the long Lenten fast with fresh green cabbage and floury potatoes. March 17 also marks the opening of salmon season in Ireland. Perhaps a nice poached salmon with Irish butter sauce would be a more elegant choice?

Sheelah's Day	March 18

Sheelah is a mysterious figure who has been identified variously as the wife, mother, or other relative of St. Patrick. Not so anxious to determine who Sheelah was as much as they were in celebrating her immortal memory, eighteenth-century Irish celebrated the day with copious amounts of whiskey. At the end of the day, the faithful would take their shamrocks and drop them in their respective glasses before downing the contents, hence the origin of the term, 'drowning the shamrock.'

SHROVE TUESDAY

Traditionally, all the eggs in the house had to be used up before Lent. When I was growing up, my father made pancakes that resembled Crépes Suzette. He rolled them very thin and we ate them sprinkled with sugar and lemon juice.

GOOD FRIDAY

Eggs laid on Good Friday were considered blessed and these, marked with crosses, were cooked for breakfast on Easter Sunday.

EASTER SUNDAY

Simnel Cake. This is a fruit cake that was introduced into Ireland by English settlers. Traditionally, it is decorated with eleven small marzipan balls, representing eleven of the twelve apostles. Judas is missing because of his betrayal.

MAY DAY   MAY 1

Nettle Soup was customarily associated with May Day or *Bealtaine* - one of the four great Celtic festivals and a celebration of the traditional first day of summer. May-pole dancing until the wee hours used to take place in many parts of Ireland, as well as the lighting of bonfires and the collecting of young stinging nettles. Children gathered them in baskets and they were made into a soup or cooked like spinach. There used to be a belief that nettles should be eaten three times during the month of May to purify the blood after winter and to keep away the rheumatics for another year.

ST. CARTHAGE	MAY 15
ST. BRENDAN	MAY 16
ST. KEVIN	JUNE 4
ST. JARLATH	JUNE 6
ST. COLMAN	JUNE 7
ST. COLUM CILLE	JUNE 9
ST. JOHN'S DAY	JUNE 21

Traditionally the day for digging up the first new potatoes. No doubt, the first batch be on the menu for dinner.

St. Kilian	July 8
St. Oliver Plunkett	July 10
St. Declan	July 24

Lughnasa	First weekend in August

This is the Irish word for August and was considered to be the most joyous of the four Celtic Festivals as it was also celebration of the harvest.

St. Nathy	August 9
St. Felim	August 9
St. Attracta	August 12
St. Lelia	August 12
St. Muredach	August 12
St. Fachanan	August 14
Assumption of Our Lady	August 15
St. Eugene	August 23
St. Fiacra	August 30.

St. Mac Nissi	September 4
St. Ciaran	September 9
St. Ailbe	September 12
St. Eunan	September 23
St. Finbarr	September 25
Michaelmas	September 29

Michaelmas Goose with Potato Apple Stuffing. *

This is the feast day of St. Michael the Archangel and it's commonly associated with geese because the birds that were hatched in the spring in May would now be mature and ready for market.

St. Canice	October 11
St. Gall	October 16
St. Thaddeus McCarthy	October 25
St. Otteran	October 27
St. Colman	October 29
Halloween	October 31

In ancient times, the Celtic Festival Samhain was celebrated on November 1, the first day of winter. When Christianity came to Ireland, the celebrations were moved to the night before. There's an old superstition that one should never eat blackberries after Halloween because the devil might have spat on them. Or worse!. The traditional dish is *Barmbrack*, a rich, fruit bread that often had various objects wrapped up and hidden in the cake mixture - a wedding ring, a coin, a pea or a thimble signifying spinsterhood. When it was time to cut the Barmbrack, everyone hoped to get the ring because it meant marriage was certain before the end of the year.

ALL SAINT'S DAY	NOVEMBER 1
ST. MALACHY	NOVEMBER 3
ALL SAINTS OF IRELAND	NOVEMBER 6
ST. MARTIN'S EVE.	NOVEMBER 10

On Martinmas - the eve of St. Martin's Day - it was traditional to kill a pig and make a feast of *Roast Pork*.

ST. LAURENCE O'TOOLE	NOVEMBER 14
ST. COLUMBANUS	NOVEMBER 23
ST. COLMAN	NOVEMBER 24
ST. FERGAL	NOVEMBER 27
ST NICHOLAS	DECEMBER 6
ST. FINNIAN	DECEMBER 12
ST. FLANNAN	DECEMBER 18
ST. FACHANAN	DECEMBER 20
CHRISTMAS	DECEMBER 25

Today, most Irish households serve turkey for Christmas dinner. They might also treat the family to oysters, especially the prized ones from Galway Bay, if they can get them.

ST. STEPHEN'S DAY	DECEMBER 26

*Spiced Beef,** served cold and sliced very thin is traditionally served on this feast day.

Note: St. Colman's Feast Day is celebrated on June 7th in the town of Dromore, and on November 24th in Cloyne.

St. Fachanan's Feast Day is celebrated on August 14th in Ross, and on December 20th in Kilfenora.

IV
PROGRAM IDEA AND FAVORS

PROGRAM DESIGN IDEA

Purchase several full sheets of heavyweight paper and have them cut into what will become 9" x 12" program covers when folded. To embellish the outside in a subtle way, emboss the lower right hand corner with your first names. A personal embosser is very reasonably priced and can be used afterwards to emboss thank-you notes and other stationery.

For the inside of the program, select complimentary color 8 1/2" x 11" letter stock sheets, which when folded, will fit inside the cover. You, or someone you know with access to a personal computer, can key in the copy for the front, center and back. For the title lines, select a Celtic style typeface and do the body copy in one that is easy to read - Times Roman, for example.

On the front, in addition to your names, you could include an Irish wedding vow. And, on the back, you could have another appropriate Irish quotation. One couple we know made extensive use of the Claddagh symbol throughout their wedding and put the legend of the Claddagh on the back of their program. It makes for absorbing reading while waiting for the ceremony to begin. To finish the program, position both the cover and center sheets together and use a hole punch to make two holes along the center folds. Then, cut a length of ribbon and thread it from the center to the outside and tie it in a bow.

Irish Symbols

Draw from Irish history and culture to get your creative juices flowing. Swans, shamrocks, St. Patrick, pots of gold, rainbows, leprechauns, harps, Irish lace, The Book of Kells, the ancient symbols at Newgrange, the Tara brooch, the Claddagh ring, the stitches on an Aran Isle sweater - all of these and many others offer endless possibilities for designing programs and creating favors. Also, if you have access to the internet, you will find many pages devoted to Celtic art.

Salt Dough Ornaments

This 'recipe' is from one of our closest friends, Janis Keating, by way of her mom, Bette. Their ancestors were from County Wexford.

These easy-to-make ornaments will net you inexpensive keepsakes that are particularly meaningful because you created them yourself.

Ingredients
4 cups plain flour
1 cup salt
1 1/4 cups water

Materials
Medium size mixing bowl/fork/rolling pin
Aluminum foil for lining cookie sheets and easy paint clean up
Paper clips, one for each ornament
Clear-drying glue
Acrylic paint(s) and paint brush(es)
Clear acrylic spray or clear varnish
1/4" wide satin ribbon in your choice of color, cut into three-inch lengths

1. Mix flour and salt with fork in mixing bowl. Add one cup of water and continue mixing until crumbly.

2. Add 1/4 cup water and knead dough until it's smooth and leathery. Be sure it's mixed thoroughly so there are no lumps. Add extra water sparingly only if dough seems to be extremely dry.

3. Use right away or store in an airtight container in refrigerator.

4. Roll out dough to about a 1/4" thick; flour your rolling pin if dough seems sticky.

5. Use cookie cutters or shape by hand and insert a paper clip dipped in clear-drying glue into the top of each ornament before baking.

6. Place ornaments on a greased or foil-lined cookie sheet.

7. Heat oven to 225°F.

8. Bake until ornaments are hard. Watch carefully - oven temperatures vary as will the desired thickness of your ornaments. For 1/4" thick dough, it can take several hours at 225°F. Plan on at least two hours and much longer if several batches are baked at the same time.

9. Remove with a spatula to cooling rack.

10. When ornaments are cooled thoroughly, move them onto a foil-lined surface for painting. If you are using several colors, allow each color to dry so that they don't smudge into each other.

11. An optional step is to write your names and wedding date on the back of each ornament. An ultra fine point permanent marker will probably work best on the hard surface.

12. When paint is thoroughly dry, spray entire ornament, front and back, with clear acrylic spray or clear varnish to seal. This is an essential step to prevent humidity from softening the baked dough.

13. Tie a three-inch length of satin ribbon through the paper clip loop.

In designing your ornaments, simple is best (and fastest!). Pick up a set of aluminum cookie cutters that includes a shamrock, heart and circle shape or purchase them individually. The shamrocks are the easiest to decorate - simply paint them green. For the hearts and circles, use your imagination to create a series of Celtic-inspired designs. Also, see the listing under Irish symbols mentioned earlier for other ideas. For a sparkly effect, you might also consider coating ornaments with clear-drying glue and sprinkling them with glitter before you spray with varnish or clear acrylic. When glue is dry and sparkles are 'set', then spray with varnish or clear acrylic.

Miniature Scrolls

We ordered packages of 144 imitation rings from a wedding stationer. We then selected 16 Irish proverbs and sayings of approximately the same length which were keyed into the computer and spaced so that we ended up with eight to a page. Each saying was keyed in so that it measured about 1 1/2" wide and three inches deep. On an 8 1/2" x 11" page, this resulted in four sayings on the top half and four on the bottom. Our guest list was 150 so we printed out 4 pages of each group. We then used a paper cutter to cut and trim them evenly, rolled them up and secured each one with an imitation wedding band. While we measured our scrolls so they would fit inside a miniature box of chocolates, how big or small you make your scrolls is entirely up to you. A larger scroll put at each place setting would generate the same response we experienced at our daughter's reception - guests eagerly comparing their sayings. Unexpectedly, the scrolls had assumed their own identity, that of an Irish fortune cookie!

Tent Cards

This idea is from Kate McLaughlin who selected a series of customs related to Irish weddings and then had them printed up on the front of blank informal note cards featuring the Claddagh symbol. She placed one on each table and, according to Kate, guests went from table to table until they had read them all.

County Cards

For her daughter's wedding reception, Eileen McTiernan 'named' each of the tables after counties that figure prominently in the history and heritage of relatives and friends. She used blank cards on which the county name was printed in a very large font called Stonehenge 58. Two copies of each card were made so that the name would be visible from both sides of the table. The cards were then given a decorative edge. Eileen also typed up a bit of background information on each county and placed it next to the card.

V
COMPILATION OF IRISH WORDS, PHRASES AND SAYINGS

A ghrá (ah ghraw - hard 'g)	My love
Anam Cara (ah-nahm khara)	Soul mate
An bpósfaidh tú mé?	Will you marry me?
(on bohs-ee thoo may?)	
A stór (ah sthohr)	Darling
Álainn (awl-yin)	Beautiful
Bainis (bah-nish)	Wedding/Reception
Barróga agus póga	
(bahrogue-ah ah-guss pogue-ah)	Hugs and kisses
Bean/Fear Chleamhnais	
(bahn/fahr khlow (as in 'cow')-nish)	Female/Male matchmaker
Breá (brah)	Handsome
Brídeach (bree-djuikh)	Bride
Cailín coimhdeachta	
(coll-een kwev-djahkh-thah)	Bridesmaid
Cóisir bhainise	Wedding Celebration
(koh-shir wahn-ish-eh)	
Croí (kree)	Heart
Cuireadh (kwirr-eh)	Invitation
Fáinne pósta (fawn-yeh phos-thah)	Wedding Ring
Fáinne gealltanais	Engagement Ring
(fawn-yeh gi-ahll-thahn-ish)	
Fear nuapósta	Bridegroom
(fahr noo-ah-fohs-thah)	
Finné fir (finn-ay fir)	Best Man
Gealltanas pósta (gih-ahl-thah-nahs)	Engagement
Grá (graw)	Love
Grá go deo (graw guh deo)	Love Forever
Grá/ titim i ngrá le	
(graw/thitch-im ih ngraw leh)	Love/Sweetheart/To fall in love with
Grá mo chroí (graw mo khree)	Love of My Heart

Lá pósta (or) bainise	
(law pohs-thah (or) bahn-ish-eh)	Wedding Day
Leannán (lih-ahn-awn)	Lover
Lucht banise (lukth bahn-ish-eh)	Bridal Party
Mí na Meala (mee nah mahlah)	Honeymoon
Mo grá thú (muh ghraw hoo)	My Love To You
Mo mhuirnín (muh voor-neen)	My Sweetheart
Póg mé (pogue may)	Kiss Me
Pósadh (pohs-ah)	Marriage
Tá cion agam ort	
(thaw kiuhn ag-gum urth)	I Love You
Thabharfainn fuil mo chroí duit	
(hohr-hinn fwill muh khree gwitch)	I'd give you the blood of my heart

A MISCELLANY OF SAYINGS

The kettle is on the boil there (something brewing between two people).

A little fire that warms is better than a big fire that burns.

Young man, you'll be troubled, 'til you marry, and from then on, you'll know no rest.

Don't ever be in court or castle without a woman to make your excuse.

Marriages are all happy. It's having breakfast together that causes all the trouble.

The old pipe gives the sweetest smoke.

Always make sure she looks beautiful before breakfast as well as after dinner.

A lad's best friend is his mother until he's the best friend of a lassie.

If she pleases the eye, she'll please the heart.

Love is like stirabout. It must be made fresh every day.

Old coals are easiest kindled.

Every thrush thinks her mate sings the sweetest.

Once you break the ice it won't be long 'til you can lift the water.

Men are like bagpipes. No sound comes from them 'til they are full.

A man is a man when his woman is a woman.

When you go forth to find a wife, leave your eyes at home but take both ears with you.

The three with the lightest hearts: a student after reading his psalms, a young lad who has left off his boy's clothes for good and a maid who has been made a woman.

Mock oath said by a girl to her sweetheart if he teased her too much: 'The divil go with you and sixpence, an' then you'll want neither money nor company!'

Ah, Tom, said she with wide eyes and a smile, if I were you and you were me, I'd have been married years ago.

It is a great pleasure entirely to be alone, especially when your sweetheart is with you.

Won't you come into the garden? I should like my roses to see you.

Courtship in Ireland is said to be that period during which a girl decides whether or not she can do any better.

Before the age of fifty-five, there is no such thing as a confirmed bachelor, only an obstinate one.

The best test of a man is his choice of a wife.

Never praise your son-in-law until the year is out.

It is better to be quarreling than lonely.

VI

RESOURCE LISTING

In the first edition of this book, I included more than a dozen pages of resources. While I thought it would be convenient, it proved to be a major problem. The listing became out-dated almost as soon as the book was published.

As the interest in Irish and Celtic wedding celebrations continues to flourish, there are now many new resources available, and a good many of them are on the internet. Since more and more people are now connected to the net, I have created a special Traditional Irish Wedding Page on my web site, Irish Culture and Customs. There, you will find a revised listing of all the resources which appeared in the first edition, as well as many new ones. Please visit the site at: www.irishcultureandcustoms.com

Remember, too, there are literally hundreds of Irish gift shops throughout North America. For a retailer near you, visit the North American Celtic Buyers Association at www.celticbuyers.com Listings are both alphabetical and by state or province.

Not everyone has access to the net, so an abbreviated listing of resources is included in this edition. What follows are the names of companies, organizations, retailers and people I found in the course of my research which may be of interest to engaged couples. I also chose to list only those resources that have a toll-free number unless they offer a unique service or product.

Have fun browsing and shopping!

BRIDAL CLOAK & HOOD
SiobhanWear: Tel: (800) 522-2917

BRIDAL GOWN DESIGNERS
Brontë Bridal Designs: Dublin, Ireland. Tel: 353-1-671-0155
Celtia Wedding Gowns: Scotland. Tel: 44-01-896-754493
Kathy De Stafford: Dublin. Ireland. Tel: 353-1-679-8817

BRIDAL GOWN FABRICS
Miriam Richards Fabrics: Dublin, Ireland. Tel: 353-1-836-7937

BRIDAL HEADPIECES, TIARAS & VEILS
Bridal Creations: Tel: (860) 747-2035
Colleen Collections: Co. Galway, Ireland. Tel: 353-907-55468
Paris Hats & Veils: Tel: (513) 948-8888

CATALOGS
The most efficient way to browse for specific items mentioned in the book is to order the following catalogs as soon as you set the date. From Claddagh rings to the Magic Wedding Hanky to Irish Linen and Lace, you should be able to find what you are looking for. You are also likely to find many additional products not mentioned that would be appropriate for an Irish wedding celebration.
Arts & Artifact: Tel: (800) 231-6766
Blarney Gifts: Tel: (800) 252-7639
Cashs' of Ireland : Tel: (800) 223-8100
Creative Irish Gifts: Tel: (800) 843-4538
Irish Dancer's Catalogue: Tel: (301) 460-0129
Past Times: Tel: (800) 621-6020
Scottish Lion Import Shops Irish Edition: Tel: (800) 355-7268
Shannon Gifts: Tel: (800) 223-6716
Signals: Tel: (800) 669-9696
Spirit of Ireland: Tel: (800) 486-4183
What On Earth: Tel: (800) 945-2552

DECORATIONS
Invitations by Dawn: Tel: (800) 332-3296
Kipp Brothers: Tel: (800) 832-5477
The Precious Collection: Tel: (800) 537-5222

FAVORS
Bags & Bows: Beautiful ribbons, tissue papers, seals and tiny boxes that are the perfect size for favors! Tel: (800) 225-8155
Fawn Confectionery: Large variety of Irish motif candies. Tel: (513) 351-4191
Hercules Candies: Claddagh- embossed and assorted other chocolates. Tel: (800) 924-4339
Swan candy holder and miniature wedding rings: Invitations by Dawn. Tel: (800) 228-4795

HONEYMOON IN IRELAND
Adams & Butler: P. O. Box 2281, Dublin 4. Tel: 353-6607-975
Cruise Co. of Greenwich: Tel: (800) 825-0826
Le Boat Inc.: Tel: (800) 992-0291
Free Irish Vacation Kit: Tel: (800) Shamrock, extension 135
Hidden Ireland: Tel: (800) 688-0299
Irish Festival Tours: If you'd rather honeymoon in the tropics but would like to be surrounded by Irish culture and entertainment, they can arrange it! Tel: (800) 441-HARP
Isle Inn Tours: Tel: (800) 237-9376. (703) 683-4800
Killary Tours: County Galway, Ireland. Tel: 353-95-42276
Mandalay: A beautiful B&B in County Galway. This is the romantic place I mention in the honeymoon chapter. It's owned and operated by the Darby's, a delightful couple from Rhode Island. To make a reservation, see your travel agent or call 353-91-524177/91-529952
Northern Ireland Tourist Board: Tel: (212) 686-6250.
Oideas Gael - Irish Language and Culture Center: For a free brochure, write to Oideas Gael, Gleann Cholm Cille, County Donegal, Ireland or call 353-73-30248.
Town & Country Homes Association: For a directory, write to Mr. Sean Grogan, St. Patricks, Corebeg, Doora, Ennis. County Clare, Ireland, or ask your travel agent.
Weddings On The Move: Tel: (800) 444-6967

INVITATIONS/PROGRAMS
Historical Irish Wedding Stationery: County Clare, Ireland.
Tel: 353-65-905-2100
Lantz Stationery Ltd.: County Dublin, Ireland.
Tel: 353-1-478-0733
Custom Invitations: Cynthia R. Matyi. Tel: (513) 871-4527

IRISH BOOK DISTRIBUTORS
Dufour Editions: Tel: (800) 869-5677

IRISH DANCE COSTUME DESIGNERS
Listowel Celtic Art: Tel: (412) 341-5826.

IRISH DANCING SCHOOLS
To locate embroiderers and Celtic dressmakers, or perhaps to
invite a group to dance at your reception, look under Dance
Instruction in your Yellow Pages phone directory in the United
States or equivalent elsewhere. Most large cities have at least one
school and many may have several. None listed in your area? If
you live in the United States, call Allison Weber Erickson TCRG,
at (513) 232-1366. Allison teaches both adults and children and is
a registered Irish dance instructor. That's what the letters after her
name signify. This also means that she is listed in a world-wide
directory of registered teachers and, if there's an instructor near
you, she will be able to give you their phone number. You can also
write her at: The Erickson Academy of Irish Dance, 6448, Sherman
Avenue, Cincinnati, OH 45230.

IRISH FESTIVALS - NORTH AMERICA
Just a sampling of the hundreds of festivals that take place every
year throughout North America. If you live near one of them, it's a
wonderful opportunity to get close to your Irish roots and browse
for jewelry, gifts, foods, music, books and more!
Cincinnati Celtic Music & Cultural Festival: Tel: (513) 533-4822
Cleveland's Irish Cultural Festival: Tel: (216) 251-1711
Dublin Irish Festival: Dublin, Ohio. Tel: (614) 410-4545
Fox Valley Irish Fest: Chicago, Illinois. Tel: (800) 788-7429

Irish Fest, Indiana: Tel: (317) 927-7524
Irish Festival: Richmond, Virginia. Tel: (804) 750-1346
Louisville Irish Festival: Tel: (812) 944-3509
Milwaukee Irish Fest: Tel: (414) 476-3378
New Orleans Irish Festival: Tel: (504) 529-1317
Taste of Ireland: Chicago, Illinois. Tel: (773) 282-7035

IRISH FOODS
Irish Breakfast:
Dairygold specializes in Shannon/Traditional Galtee Irish breakfasts.
Tel: (800) 386-7577
Irish Cheeses, Oak-Smoked Salmon and other foods imported from Ireland:
Dean & DeLuca: Tel: (800) 221-7714
Infood: Tel: (201) 569-3175
Irish Dairy Board: Tel: (708) 256-8289
Irish Food Distributors: Tel: (800) 366-3773
Zingeman's: Tel: (313) 769-1625
Specialty Foods:
Bewley Irish Imports: Tel: (610) 696-2682
For more information on Irish foods available in North America,
call the Irish Food Board at (212) 207-1920

IRISH GIFT SHOPS
There are literally hundreds of Irish gift shops throughout the
United States and Canada. For a retailer near you, visit the North
American Celtic Buyers Association website at
www.celticbuyers.com

IRISH MAGAZINES & NEWSPAPERS
A great source for ads on everything from jewelry to car rentals in
Ireland! These are the ones with which I am most familiar; there
are many others.
Ireland of the Welcomes: Tel: (800) 876-6336
Irish America: Tel: (800) 341-1522
Irish American Post: Tel: (414) 283-8132
Irish American News: Tel: (708) 445-0700
Irish Voice: Tel: (800) 341-1522

IRISH MASSES (Recorded)
Public Radio Music Source: If it's in print, (both music and videos), they'll find it for you! This is where we found the Gaelic Blessing from the CD, Gloria by John Rudder, *St Patrick's Mass* by Philip Green, *The Mass of St. Francis of Assisi* by Philip Green, *Celtic Hymns,* and *The Contemplative Celt.* They no longer accept enquiries or orders by telephone, but are on the internet at www.prms.org

IRISH MASSES (Sheet Music)
Oregon Catholic Press can provide the sheet music and a sampling tape of *The Celtic Mass* by Christopher Walker.
Tel: (800) 548-8749

IRISH MEADE
Bunratty Wine & Spirits: Camelot Importing.
Tel: (800) 422-6356. Ask for Nancy Larkin Rau - she's very friendly as well as helpful.

IRISH MUSIC (Recorded)
NARADA MEDIA: Tel: (800) 966-3699
Rego Irish Records & Tapes: On the web at www.regorecords.com

IRISH WEDDING COORDINATORS
Maria Curran: Dublin. Tel: 353-1-851-1141
Tara Fay: Dublin.Tel: 353-1-667-5858
Brigid Horne-Nestor: Cincinnati, OH. Tel (513) 762-5550
Helen Russell: Dublin. Tel: 353-1- 820-9198

IRISH WEDDING SONG (Sheet music)
Rego Records stocks *The Wedding Song Book* which contains the music and lyrics to *The Irish Wedding Song* as well several other songs often played at Irish weddings. On the web at www.regorecords.com

LUCKY IRISH FIVE-PENNY PIECE
Available from most Irish gift shops: The five-penny piece we bought is from a company called 'The Bridget's of Erin,' and comes in a tiny satin and embroidered keepsake pouch.

OGHAM ALPHABET
New Age Canada: Ogham divining sticks with alphabet key.
Tel: (905) 271-0967

ST. PATRICK, MISSOURI POST MARK
St. Patrick Post Office: 2 Erin Circle, Saint Patrick, MO, 63466.
Tel: (660)-754-6511

WEDDINGS IN IRELAND
Anne Lanier Weddings: www.annelanierweddings.com
Killary Tours: They can arrange a total package, including
ceremony, lodging for you and your guests, and your
honeymoon. Killary Lodge, County. Galway, Ireland.
Tel: 353 0 95 42302
Weddings On The Move: They specialize in planning and
coordinating all of the details that go into getting married
overseas.Tel: (800) 444-6967

WEDDINGS IN ROME
St. Patrick's Irish National Church: Tel: 39-06-4203-121. It is best to
phone between 4.00 pm and 6.00 pm; or between 7.30 pm and
9.30 pm, Irish time

IMPORTANT NOTE: While very effort has been made to check the accuracy of names, addresses and phone numbers, information may change and products or services mentioned may no longer be available. I apologize for any inconvenience or disappointment. For the most up-to-date and more detailed listing of resources, please consult my website: www.irishcultureandcustoms.com

VII

NOTES AND BIBLIOGRAPHY

A book such as this involves a lot of reading and research. Many customs and traditions exist in various versions and some continue to exist in the oral tradition. While it's impossible to list every source for each, I have tried to make certain that my main references - those books and their authors that I referred to over and over again - receive full credit for their invaluable contribution to this work. You'll find them listed under Select Bibliography. Most of these books are now a precious part of my own personal library and if you'd like to learn more about your Irish heritage, they're a great place to begin.

NOTES TO THE CHAPTERS

If a book does not appear here, it is given full bibliographical reference in the select bibliography.

Acknowledgements
W.B. Yeats quotation is from *The Municipal Gallery Revisited* and appears in *A Little Book of Irish Quotations* compiled by Sean McMahon

1. According To Custom
Skellig poem from *English as We Speak It in Ireland* by P. W. Joyce
St. Patrick's Day 'luckiest day to wed' and saying from *Tying the Celtic Knot*, an article by Jesse Knadler published in *The Irish Voice*, February 12, 1997.
Irish quotation from *Ireland in Love* by Anthony Bluett.
Verse from 'The Queen of Love' from James N. Healy's *Book of Irish Street Ballads* reprinted in *Irish in Love* by Anthony Bluett.
County Wexford quotation from *How the Irish Speak English* by Padraic O'Farrell.
Magpie quotation from *English as We Speak It in Ireland* by P. W. Joyce.
The phrase *d'réir an seana chultúr* is from the glossary of terms which

appear in Eamon Kelly's book, *In My Father's Time*
Five volumes of Brehon law tracts have been translated into English
and while it is a monumental work, historians caution that it
contains many faulty readings and the translations are not always
trustworthy. Source for information related to the Brehon Laws is
Sex and Marriage in Ancient Ireland by Patrick C. Power.
Metal Man custom from *Ireland In Love* by Anthony Bluett.
County Westmeath 'jumping the bezum' custom from *How The Irish
Speak English* by Padraic O'Farrell.
Chalk Sunday reference from *English As We Speak It in Ireland* by P.W.
Joyce.
Trysting Stone custom from *The Man From Cape Clear* by Conchér Ó
Siocháin.
Dingle Ogham stone custom from *The Irish Wedding Book* by Kim
McGuire.
The Maiden's Plight by Brian Merriman from *The Book of Irish Verse*
selected and introduced by John Montague.
Reference to a pre-wedding celebration in the old days from *The Irish
Wedding Book* by Kim McGuire.
Superstition about breaking a cup or glass from *Things Irish* by
Anthony Bluett.
Superstition about washing hands in the same sink from *The Irish
Wedding Book* by Kim McGuire.
Wedding chest custom from *In Ireland Long Ago* by Kevin Danaher.
Proverb on courtship from *Proverbs and Sayings of Ireland,* eds Gaffney
and Cashman.
Wedding portents and signs from *In Ireland Long Ago* by
Kevin Danaher.
Skellig Lists from *English As We Speak It In Ireland* by
P.W. Joyce.
Lough Derg pilgrimage information from *A Day in the Life of Ireland.*

2. Irish Wedding Stories
For the sources of these stories, please see Select Bibliography.
County Galway custom of lighting fires along the road
contributed by Síle O'Connor.
O Lady Fair verse from John Montague's version of the poem, *The
Wooing of Etain*, which appears in the *Book of Irish Verse*, selected and

edited by the same author.
Reference to human-hair bracelet from *Strange Customs of Courtship and Marriage* by William J. Fielding.

3. From Attire to Transportation
Sir Samuel Ferguson quotation from *A Little Book of Irish Quotations* by Sean McMahon.
The Bride She Bound Her Golden Hair from *Sir Turlough or the Churchyard Bride* by William Carleton.
Marriage divination poem from *Ireland in Love* by Anthony Bluett.
Irish Quotation from *Gems of Irish Wisdom: Irish Proverbs and Sayings* by Padraic O'Farrell.
Poem about a woman's clothing from *The Midnight Court* by Brian Merriman and translated by Cosslett Ó Cuinn.
'Shingerleens' from *English as We Speak It in Ireland* by P.W. Joyce.
Quotation about embroidery from *The Little Book of Celtic Wisdom* compiled by John and Caitlin Matthews.
Idea for carrying an heirloom family handkerchief from *Irish Wedding Traditions* by Shannon McMahon-Lichte
Heraldic historical information from the Claddagh Jewellers brochure.
Reference about brides carrying herbs in their bouquets from 'Celtic Traditions' compiled by Celtia Wedding Gowns.
All of the following references are from Tara Fay, one of Ireland's foremost wedding coordinators: Superstition about birthstone in the engagement ring, and superstitions about earrings, tearing your wedding gown, a married woman putting on your veil and about looking at the sun when you leave for your wedding.
Rules about the groom not seeing the bride and the bride not seeing her full reflection in the mirror from www.weddingsireland.com.

4. Pre-Wedding Parties
Pickin' the gander reference from *Land of My Cradle Days* by Martin Morrissey.
Jack Mullowney's potthalowng from *English as We Speak It in Ireland*

by P.W. Joyce.

Reference to handball from *Things Irish* by Anthony Bluett .

Reference to road bowling (Ibid).

Walking the land custom from *Of Irish Ways* by Mary Murray Delaney.

5. Ceremony

Charm to win love from *A Treasury Of Irish Folklore* edited by Padraic Colum.

Superstition about singing from *In Ireland Long Ago* by Kevin Danaher.

Galway custom of lighting fires along the road contributed by Síle O'Connor.

Prayers when going to and leaving Mass from *Of Irish Ways* by Mary Murray Delaney.

St Patrick's Breastplate from T*reasury of Irish Folklore* edited by Padraic Colum who took it from *Selections from Ancient Irish Poetry* translated by Kuno Meyer.

Prayer for protection from *Land of My Cradle Days* by Martin Morrissey.

Blessing for a Bride and Groom from *The Little Book of Celtic Blessings* translated by Caitlin Matthews.

Blessing for a lover from *Carmina Gadelica*, vol 3.

A Druid Blessing for Unity from *The Druid Way* by Philip Carr-Gomm.

A Morning Blessing from Conrad Bladey's Irish Studies Pages.

Irish Wedding Vows from *The Religious Songs of Connacht* translated by Douglas Hyde.

Irish Blessing from Conrad Bladey's Irish Studies Pages.

Maiden name reference from *Of Irish Ways* by Mary Murray Delaney

Superstition about wishing the bride joy (Ibid).

Reference about young men carrying torches of bogwood from 'Celtic Traditions' compiled by Celtia Wedding Gowns.

6. Reception

Tradition about where weddings were held from *In Ireland Long Ago* by Kevin Danaher.

Hot drinks reference from *In Ireland Long Ago* by Kevin Danaher.

Reference to kish (basket) from *Of Irish Ways* by Mary Murray Delaney.

Reference to wedding cake charm symbols from *Things Irish* by Anthony Bluett.

Blessing before a meal from *The Religious Songs of Connacht* translated by Douglas Hyde.

Other blessings from *Irish Blessings* compiled by Pat Fairon.

Blessing from *Before the Devil Knows You're Dead* by Padraic O'Farrell.

The Heavenly Banquet poem is attributed to St. Brigid. There are several versions and this one is from Conrad Bladey's Irish Studies Pages.

Revised lyrics to *The Irish Wedding Song* kindly provided by the songwriter, Ian Betteridge.

Belly bachelor from *How The Irish Speak English* by Padraic O'Farrell.

Story about mummers from *English as We Speak It In Ireland* by P.W. Joyce.

Sonoohar (Ibid).

Bacachs or strawboys reference from *Land of My Cradle Days* by Martin Morrissey.

Reference to 'Clootie' custom contributed by Marty & Cindy Shanahan of Chicago.

7. Post Wedding Parties

Scattering reference from the 1996 Milwaukee Irish Fest program.

Hauling home custom from *Land of My Cradle Days* by Martin Morrissey.

Custom about Bride's Sunday from *Of Irish Ways* by Mary Murray Delaney.

Toasts for post-wedding parties compiled by Tom Donaghue from contributions to a general toasts web site.

Custom about bride arriving at her new home from *The Man from Cape Clear* by Conchúr Ó Siocháin.

8. A Honeymoon in Ireland

Oh Ireland Isn't It Grand You Look from *The Exile's Return* by John Locke .

The 'Realm of Romance' phrase by Cleo Kilbride from an article published by The Irish Tourist Board in *Ireland of the Welcomes* magazine.

Information on accommodations in Ireland from an article by Gerry O'Connor, president of the Irish Hotels Federation, published in *Visitor Magazine.*

Story about honeymoon couple from *According to Custom* by Eamon Kelly.

Invocation from the Conquest of the Sons of Mil by Amergin from Conrad Bladey's Irish Studies Pages.

Doggerel quotation from *Western Landscape* by Louis MacNiece and reprinted in *A Little Book of Irish Quotations* compiled by Sean McMahon, Appletree Press, Belfast, 1994.

Dear Erin quotation from *Cushla Ma Chree* by John Philpot Curran (Ibid).

Erin the Tear from the poem of the same name by Thomas Moore (Ibid).

Love pact contributed by Judith Flynn who got it from the Heartwarmer's website.

NOTES TO INFORMATION & RESOURCES

I. Music
Irish Wedding Song by Ian Betteridge, from *The Wedding Song Book* arranged by Noel Healy.

II. Recipes
St. John's Feast Day reference from *Things Irish* by Anthony Bluett.
Caragh Lodge Wedding Cake from *The Best of Breads & Baking* by Georgina Campbell.

III. Saints' Feast Days
All of the entries for Irish Saints is from a compilation by Michael J. Breen which is on the Catholic Online web site.

IV. Compilation of Irish words, phrases and sayings
This collection was compiled from a number of different sources including *English As We Speak It In Ireland* by P.W. Joyce, *How The Irish Speak* English by Padraic O'Farrell, and Siobhan & Liam of Odeas Gael in Donegal.

SELECT BIBLIOGRAPHY

Allen, Darina. *The Festive Food of Ireland*. Colorado: Roberts Rinehart. 1992.
Bluett, Anthony. *Ireland In Love*. Dublin: Mercier Press. 1995.
Bluett, Anthony. *Things Irish*. Dublin: Mercier Press.1994.
Campbell, Georgina. *The Best of Irish Breads & Baking*. Dublin: Wolfhound Press. 1996.
Campbell, Georgina. *Classic Irish Recipes*. New York: Sterling Publishing Company. 1991.
Cashman, Seamus & Gaffney, Sean. *Proverbs & Sayings of Ireland*. Dublin: Wolfhound Press 1974, current edition, 1996.
Colum, Padraic. Colum. *A Treasury of Irish Folklore*. New Jersey: Random House Value Publishing. 1982.
Danaher, Kevin. *In Ireland Long Ago*. Dublin: Mercier Press. 1964.
Delaney, Mary Murray. *Of Irish Ways*. Minneapolis: Dillon Press. 1973.
Desmond, Sean. *A Touch of the Irish*. New York: QBC. 1995.
Fairon, Pat. *Irish Blessings*. San Francisco. Chronicle Books. 1993.
Fielding, William J. *Strange Customs of Courtship and Marriage*. Omnigraphics. 1995.
Healy, James N. *Love Songs of The Irish*. Dublin: Mercier Press. 1977.
Irish Proverbs and Blessings. The Sexton Company.
Irish Blessings & Sayings. The Shamrock Gift Shop.
Irish Toasts. Chronicle Books, San Francisco, 1987
Johnson, Margaret. *Cooking With Irish Spirits*. Dublin: Wolfhound Press. 1991.
Joyce, P.W. *English As We Speak It in Ireland*. Dublin: Wolfhound Press. 1988.
Keane, John B. *Letters of a Matchmaker*. Dublin: Mercier Press. 1975.
Kelly, Eamon. *According To Custom*. Dublin: Mercier Press. 1986.
Kelly, Eamon. *In My Father's Time*. Mercier Press. Dublin: 1976.
MacManus, Seumas. *The Story of The Irish Race*. New York: Random House Value Publishing.1990.
Matthews, Caitlin. *The Little Book of Celtic Blessings*. Massachusetts: Element Books Ltd. 1994.
Matthews, John & Caitlin. *The Little Book of Celtic Wisdom*. Massachusetts: Element Books Ltd. 1993.

McGuire, Kim. *The Irish Wedding Book.* Dublin: Wolfhound Press. 1994.

McMahon-Lichte, Shannon. *Irish Wedding Traditions.* New York: Hyperion. 2001

McMahon, Sean. *A Little Book of Irish Quotations.* Belfast: The Appletree Press, Ltd. 1994.

Montague, John. *The Book of Irish Verse.* New York: Galahad Books. 1974.

Morrissey, Martin. *Land of My Cradle Days.* Dublin: O'Brien Press Ltd. 1990.

Ó Conchúrm Siocháinm. *The Man From Cape Clear.* Dublin: Mercier Press 1933

O'Farrell, Padraic. *How The Irish Speak English.* Dublin: Mercier Press. 1993.

O'Farrell, Padraic. *Before the Devil Knows You're Dead.* Dublin. Mercier Press. 1993.

Power, Patrick C. *Sex and Marriage in Ancient Ireland.* Dublin: Mercier Press. 1993.

Walton's Manufacturing Ltd. *Ireland's Best Loved Songs and Ballads.* Massachusetts: Walton's Music, Inc. 1988.

FOR PERSONAL NOTES

FOR PERSONAL NOTES

FOR PERSONAL NOTES

FOR PERSONAL NOTES

FOR PERSONAL NOTES

FOR PERSONAL NOTES

FOR PERSONAL NOTES

FOR PERSONAL NOTES

FOR PERSONAL NOTES

FOR PERSONAL NOTES